ABORIGINAL FABLES

AND LEGENDARY TALES

Every day begins with laughter.
(*From* Laughing Jackass and the Sun Fire.)

ABORIGINAL FABLES

AND LEGENDARY TALES

by

A. W. REED

Author of *Myths and Legends of Australia*

illustrated by

E. H. PAPPS

A. H. & A. W. REED

SYDNEY - WELLINGTON - AUCKLAND

First published 1965

A. H. & A. W. REED
143-5 York Street, Sydney
182 Wakefield Street, Wellington
St Paul Street, Auckland

Also in this series
Aboriginal Words of Australia

Printed in Great Britain by C. Tinling & Co. Ltd.,
Liverpool, London and Prescot.

INTRODUCTION

LIVING close to nature and dependent on his powers of observation for survival, the Australian aborigine might well be expected to have manufactured a number of myths and legends to account for the origin of animals, birds, insects, reptiles, and fish, and for their behaviour and appearance; but to those who are not familiar with aboriginal folklore it comes as a surprise to discover how many of these stories have been inherited by the various tribes. Even more surprising is the wealth of imagination, the sense of humour, the ingenuity and variety of the camp fire tales that have been told and retold for hundreds of years in different parts of Australia.

The Dreamtime, that happy period of earlier days, is well known. It was a halcyon era when the world, and mankind, and all created things, were young. There was a natural innocence in this period when animals were still like men. The interchange of form between man and animal is often puzzling, and there are times when we cannot be sure whether the hero or the villain of a story is a man or an animal. Often enough, of course, the purpose of the tale is to relate how the animal gained its special characteristics and changed from a two-legged mammal to a bird, a lizard, or an animal. More important still is the connection with the origins of totemism, which was such an important feature of family and tribal life.

The collection of fables and folk tales in this book is confined to shorter myths and legends, and especially to those which provide an imaginative explanation of animal life and natural phenomena. If they succeed in interesting others in the heritage that the earlier inhabitants of Australia have handed down to us, the compiler will be well rewarded. All the stories have previously appeared in print but have been retold for this collection. The fables which have been retold in this book appeared originally in the titles following. Where there are several different versions of a legend in various books, the accounts have been compared. In a few cases the story may therefore be of a composite character and not confined to a single tribe. The fables have been told by many different tribes over a wide area and in the majority of cases cannot be allocated to a single source.

Attenborough, David. *Quest Under Capricorn*. Lutterworth Press. 1963.

Barrett, Charles. *The Bunyip*. Reed and Harris. 1946.

Bell, Enid. *Legends of the Coochin Valley*. Bunyip Press. N.D.

Guirand, Felix. *Larousse Encyclopaedia of Mythology*. Paul Hamlyn. 1962.

Gunn, Mrs Aeneas. *The Little Black Princess*. Robertson and Mullens Ltd and Angus and Robertson Ltd.

Harney, W. E. (Bill). *Tales from the Aborigines*. Robert Hale. 1959.

McConnel, Ursula. *Myths of the Munkan*. Melbourne University Press. 1957.

McKeown, Keith C. *Insect Wonders of Australia*. Angus and Robertson Ltd. 1944.

The Land of Byamee. Angus and Robertson Ltd. 1938.

Marshall, Alan. *People of the Dream Time*. Cheshire. 1952.

Mathews, R. H. *Folklore of the Australian Aborigines*. Hennessey Harper and Co. Ltd. 1899.

Parker, Mrs K. Langloh. *Australian Legendary Tales*. (Selected by H. Drake-Brockman.) Angus and Robertson Ltd.

Paxton, Peter. *Bush and Billabong*. Alliance Press Ltd. 1950.

Smith, W. Ramsay. *Myths and Legends of the Australian Aboriginals*. G. G. Harrap & Co. Ltd. 1930.

Thomas, W. E. *Some Myths and Legends of the Australian Aborigines*. Whitcombe and Tombs Ltd. 1923.

Tindale, Norman and Lindsay, H. A. *Aboriginal Australians*. Jacaranda Press. 1963.

Wells, Ann E. *Rain in Arnhem Land*. Angus and Robertson Ltd. 1961.

A. W. REED

CONTENTS

7

A DARING thought once came to Yooneeara of the Kamilaroi tribe.

"I am going on a long journey towards the setting sun," he told his people. "I will not stop until I come to the home of Baiame himself."

He gathered his hunting spears, put a few possessions in his dilly bag and, as an afterthought, stuffed a live bandicoot in with his snares and fire sticks.

"What do you want to take a bandicoot with you for?" his friends asked. "Don't you think you'll be able to get enough food by hunting?"

"You never know," said Yooneeara. "It might come in useful."

He set out on his adventure and travelled for several days until he came to the land of the Dhinnabarrada, the queer men who have legs and feet like emus. They hunt together in bands looking for grubs, which are their sole food, and spend the rest of their time making boomerangs from the strong-scented wood of gidyer trees.

As soon as they saw Yooneeara they rushed towards him, trying to touch his feet, because if they had been able to do this they would have changed him into a Dhinnabarrada like themselves. They ran so quickly that the young man knew he could not escape. He put his dilly bag on the ground and opened it. The bandicoot struggled free and ran away as fast as it could. The Dhinnabarradas whooped with excitement as they gave chase, for they had never seen such a strange animal before, and Yooneeara was able to creep away unseen.

Presently he came to a large plain which was the home of the Dheeyabery tribe. When seen from in front they looked like men, but from behind they had the appearance of round balls. They gathered round the explorer and patted him with their hands.

"Where are you going?" they asked him.

Yooneeara was afraid that if they kept on feeling him with their hands he would become as round as they were.

"I am going to see Baiame," he said shortly, shook himself free, and ran away.

"Come back, come back.

Stay with us," they cried until he could no longer hear their voices.

But though he ran very fast he could not get rid of the mosquitoes and march flies that began to swarm round him. The faster he ran the more viciously they attacked him. He sank down breathless beside a water hole, but the insects attacked him until he was nearly desperate. He knew that he must protect himself or he would be driven mad. It was worse than any of the ordeals he had had to endure in the bora rite.

He took his knife and cut a large rectangle of bark from a tree; in it he made two tiny holes for eye-pieces. He wrapped it round his body and pulled the ends together as tight as he could, pushing leaves and grass into the gaps of the home-made armour. Well protected from the insects, he walked onwards towards the setting sun. Some of the insects found their way inside the armour, but they were few and he felt he could endure their bites.

After a long time the pests were left behind and he was able to take off the uncomfortable garment. He put it into a large water hole to soak, thinking that it would be soft when he returned, and that he would be able to wrap it more closely round him. As he placed it in position he noticed that the water was clear. At the bottom of the pool he saw tiny men walking about. He could hear their silvery voices calling, "Where are you?" and every now and then he saw one of them catch a fish and throw it up so that it jumped out of the water and fell on the bank.

"Thank you, little men," he said with a grin, gathered the fish into his dilly bag, and went on.

There was no need for him to spend time in hunting. His dilly bag was full of fish and he knew that he must be getting close to Kurrilwan, the home of Baiame. He passed the Weebullabulla, the misshapen old women who live on yams and lizards and have nothing to do with men, and came to the great swamp called Kollioroogla. It was not very wide, but its ends stretched to the far horizons.

At last Yooneeara's heart failed him. He could see no way of crossing the barrier. He dug his spear into the thick black mud. It sank so far down that he had difficulty in pulling it out. The swamp was too muddy to swim and too deep to walk through. He lay down to rest and slept all through the night and far into the next day. When he woke the sun was sinking behind the mountains on the far side of the swamp, and the red glow beckoned him on. He ran along the bank until he came to a fallen tree. It was long and slender, and he wondered whether it would bear his weight, but at least it was a bridge. He ran across it lightly without missing his footing, climbed the hills, and came to the far slopes of the mountains.

The place was a wonderland, lit by a sun which never sank. Game of all kinds, including animals he had never seen before, ran through the scrub, the air was filled with the singing of birds, and there was a sweet scent of flowers. The trees were all green and pointing in one direction towards a huge cave in the mountainside. At his feet a stream chuckled over the rocks and fell in a silver sheet of water into a lagoon where swans and ducks were swimming, and plants dipped their blossoms into the cool water. He ran down to the lagoon and plunged into it, washing the dust and sweat of his journey from his face and body. The water was soothing and invigorating. Yooneeara left his weapons on the bank and ran up to the cave. In front of it Byallaburragan, Baiame's daughter, was roasting a snake at a fire.

"I have been waiting for you," she said, and gave him a tender morsel of flesh, which satisfied his hunger.

"Have you come here to see my father?" she asked.

"Yes. It has been a long journey, but my soul told me to come to see the Great Spirit."

"You can see his body there," Byallaburragan told him. "It is many moons since any man has been bold enough to look at Baiame. He is asleep and you must not wake him. Look!"

Yooneeara peered into the cave. In the shadows he saw the body of a man stretched out on a bed of compressed bushes. He was many times the size of an ordinary man, and mystical patterns in white and yellow clay were painted on his body. Yooneeara longed to speak to him, but Byallaburragan warned him that it was time to leave.

"Have courage," she said, "and soon you will see him properly."

The homeward journey took many days. There was a lightness in the traveller's heart that took him quickly past all the dangers. The garment of bark was soft when he took it from the water. It clung to his body and protected him against the march flies and the mosquitoes.

Eventually he reached his home and tried to gather his people round him to tell them what had happened to him.

Yooneeara did not realise that the time he had spent in the presence of the sleeping Baiame had changed him. In a little while he died, and his spirit went direct to the Great Spirit in the land of everlasting life without having to endure the sorrows of the path.

But this was not known to Yooneeara's people. All they knew was that they would never dare to try to find the home of Baiame while blood and breath still stirred in their bodies.

THE ANGER OF PUND-JIL

AFTER the great flood, men and women became very numerous on earth. They were to be found everywhere. Wherever they went they did cruel and evil things to the animals that had been made to share the earth with them.

Then the great god Pund-jil was angry. First he made fierce storms and winds which drove the men and women into caves and valleys, where they tried in vain to shelter from the wrath of the god. Trees were blown over, and clouds of sand choked the people so that they could hardly breathe.

While they were lying on the ground struggling for breath, or crouching at the far end of caves, Pund-jil came down from the sky, armed with his huge flint knife. With it he cut those people up into little pieces, so that they no longer looked like men and women.

But that was not the end of them. Pund-jil knew who were good and who were bad. The good ones he saved. He called on the wind to carry them up into the sky, where they became stars.

And what of the bad ones? The pieces that had been men and women fell to the ground and wriggled like worms. They were blown away by wind, far into the sky, where some of them drifted down like snowflakes and melted, and were never seen again. Others were lifted up by the clouds and carried all over the world.

"Put these here," and "Put these there," Pund-jil commanded, and at his word the clouds deposited their burdens wherever Pund-jil said. Far away from their friends and families, the wandering pieces of mankind were turned into men and women again when they touched the earth. Their descendants have forgotten what happened in those far-off days, but they had better be careful lest Pund-jil should come to earth again and send them far away from their own hunting grounds.

BAIAME'S GIFT OF MANNA

For his delectation Baiame endued certain gum trees with the power to form buumbuul, or manna. This sweet substance was like lumps or bags of sugar which hung on the leaves and twigs. It could be eaten raw, or mixed with acacia gum and hot water to make a refreshing drink. Baiame warned the men and women who lived in those far off days that the trees were sacred, and must never be touched.

The women resented the prohibition. They longed to taste the food of the gods, but the men respected Baiame's orders and refused to allow them to touch the buumbuul or even to go near the trees. Baiame was aware of their temptation, and of their strength of character in resisting it.

"As a reward for your steadfastness," he told them, "I will give the buumbuul to you as a food. Look on the coolabah and bibbil trees and you will find that the food that was reserved for the gods has now been given to men."

There was great joy when the sweet food of the gods was made freely available to men and women. Year after year it was gathered and eaten, and was the most highly esteemed of all foods.

There came a time when the supplies were so plentiful that the sugar ran down the bark of the trees and hardened into large lumps. It was another sign of the tenderness of the Great One because, shortly afterwards, a great drought came to the land. Mankind might not have survived had not Baiame given them his own food with such a prodigal hand.

So it is that when the buum-buul is found in greater quantities than usual, men know that a long drought will come to the land.

BEES AND HONEY

ALTHOUGH the native bee is no bigger than a fly, it is an important provider of honey. Once the nest is found the sugar bag is eagerly devoured—wax, honey, pupae, dead bees, ants, and all. The stick which is used to pry the sugar bag from the tree is thrown in the fire, and by this simple act the spirits of the bees return to the heavens, the Paradise of the Spirits, where they stay until Mayra, the wind of spring, breathes life into the flowers again. Then the bees return to the Paradise of earth and gather honey to fill the bellies of mankind.

Bees do not think that they were created simply to provide food for men and women. Their busy lives are devoted to gathering honey and storing it up for the next generation, and therefore their nests are well hidden amongst the branches and in the hollow trunks of trees. The aborigines have several methods of discovering where the nests are hidden, but perhaps the most ingenious is the way that was first discovered by the brothers Naberayingamma.

These two Numerji men lived a long time ago. They were bearded giants who went on a long walkabout through the land. They had never seen bees until they came to a bloodwood tree where the little creatures were busily engaged in their work.

"Here is a wonderful thing," the younger brother said. "The insects are scooping honey out of the flowers and flying away with it. I wonder where they are taking it."

"We will soon find out," the elder brother said. "I will show you how to discover their nest. When we find it there will be plenty of honey for both of us. Go and cut a forked stick and bring it to me."

The younger brother had learnt to trust his brother's sagacity. While he was looking for a suitable branch, the other found a leaf which contained the cocoon of a spider. He teased out the web, and when his brother returned with the stick, he used it to climb up into the branches of the bloodwood tree.

"I am going to put bits of the web on the bees," he called out to his brother. "You will be able to see them clearly now. Watch where they go."

For some time he was busy attaching tiny fragments of spider web to the bees he managed to catch.

Presently his brother came running back.

"I have found it," he shouted. "They fly into a hollow tree down there. That's where the nest must be."

The elder Naberayingamma climbed down, and together the brothers went to the hollow tree. They broke the bark with their clubs, chopped out the honey bag, and ate it greedily.

From their discovery the aborigines learned the art of attaching a tiny white scrap of web or some other easily distinguishable piece of material to the honey bees to guide them to their nests.

BLACK PAINT AND RED OCHRE

THERE were many skilled hunters in the tribe, but none so daring as Kudnu and Wulkinara. The men were close friends and usually went in search of game together. It is said that they could think each other's thoughts. There is no doubt that constant practice enabled each to know what the other was thinking. Thus they could work and hunt together with greater success than other men. A time came when the ability to work together was the saving of the whole tribe.

Into the territory of Ngadjuri there came an old woman with

angry eyes, fingers like the talons of a bird, and sharp, pointed teeth that could tear the throat out of a man before he had time to defend himself. Alone she would have struck terror into the hearts of men, but with her two dogs, one red and the other black, she was able to roam where she wished and none dared oppose her. The dogs were like their mistress, unafraid of man or beast, and as eager as she for the taste of human blood. When several men had been torn limb from limb trying to stop the bloodthirsty trio, the whole tribe packed their possessions and began to move southward.

"Where are you going?" Kudnu demanded. "Do you think you can escape the woman by shifting to a new water hole?"

"Will you leave your territory to her simply because she lifts her lip and snarls at you?" Wulkinara asked. "Doesn't the land that belonged to your fathers mean more to you than this?"

"You haven't seen her," one of the warriors replied shamefacedly. "I would rather face a bunyip alone and in the dead of night than that old woman."

"Her dogs are monsters," another said. "If you fought with one, the other would leap on your back and crush your head in its jaws."

"I know!" a third interrupted as Kudnu was about to speak. "You are going to say that if you fought with one of the dogs, Wulkinara would guard your back . . . but what of the woman herself? No one can overcome her."

"Well, we shall see," Kudnu said with a bitter laugh. "You had better hurry or you won't catch up with the women."

The two friends looked at each other. There was no need

16

to discuss the matter. They knew what they had to do. They emerged from the scrub and stood in full view on the plain. From far away there came a distant sound of barking and two tiny dots moved towards them, rapidly growing larger as they covered the ground with huge bounds.

"Hurry up," said Wulkinara, and helped his friend into the branches of a tree, and then hid behind a low bush. Kudnu shouted as the dogs ran past the tree. They wheeled round and scrabbled at the trunk, jumping up and falling back. Wulkinara clung firmly to the branches, looking down into their open throats, marvelling at the contrast in the colour of their fur. One was a vivid red, the other jet black.

With their attention concentrated on Wulkinara, Kudnu stepped out of his hiding place with two boomerangs in his left hand. He took one in the other hand and threw it unhurriedly but with great force at the red dog. The whirling stick severed the dog's head and sent it rolling over on the sand. The black dog whirled round, caught sight of the hunter, and leapt at his throat. Wulkinara had no time to throw his weapon, but he brought it down on the dog's body with all his might, and broke the back of the black beast. The force of the blow cut the dog in two. For a moment the separate halves balanced on their front and hind legs and then collapsed.

There was rustling in the scrub. Wulkinara turned and saw the old woman leaping at him, her face contorted with rage. The man had no time to lift his boomerang, but the woman faltered in mid-air and crashed on to her back with the shaft of Kudnu's spear quivering in her throat.

The friends exchanged glances. There was no need for them to speak. Together they had done what they set out to do, and the ancestral territory was safe for their people once more. The body of the old woman was burnt, but the dogs were buried. Do not forget them, for the place where they were interred was later known because of the vast deposits of red ochre and black clay which are used by men to paint their bodies.

THE CANNIBAL WOMAN

THE old blind woman Prupe lived a lonely existence in her own small encampment. Her nearest neighbour was her sister Koromarange, who had taken charge of her granddaughter Koakangi and guarded her day and night. Her heart was heavy because she carried a secret that she was ashamed to reveal to anyone. Her sister Prupe had become a cannibal. The blind woman was too frail to hurt grown men and women, but whenever she had an opportunity she stole small children, stifling their cries with her bony hands and carrying them to her lonely camp fire where she killed them and cooked the tiny bodies as though they were wallabies or emus.

Koromarange had seen their bones scattered round her sister's camp. Becoming suspicious, she had shadowed Prupe one night, and before she could interfere she had experienced the horror of seeing one of her own grandchildren killed. It explained at once what had happened to the other grandchildren whom everyone thought had been stolen by evil spirits.

Koromarange begged her daughter to allow her to take the last remaining grandchild to her camp. The parents were about to leave on a hunting expedition and they accepted the offer with alacrity. During the day Koromarange led the little girl far away from the camp and spent the time hunting for roots and witchetty grubs. This happened every day, but she was so frightened that her sister might learn of the presence of Koakangi that she took presents of food to the blind woman to prevent her coming to visit her camp.

Unfortunately she defeated her own purpose because Prupe, to whom blindness had brought a sixth sense, realised that her sister was concealing something from her. At night she groped her way through the scrub until she could feel the heat from Koromarange's camp fire on her face. Stepping cautiously through the bushes, her fingers fluttered as delicately as the wings of a moth, feeling the body of her sister and the arm that was clasped protectively round the girl's body.

"Ah ha!" the old woman muttered as she huddled over

her camp fire later in the night. "It was Koromarange's granddaughter! She needn't think she can escape me. I'll steal her when my sister goes to the well to fetch water. I'll take her eyes and then I'll be able to see again."

Before dawn she was concealed in the bushes. As soon as she heard her sister going to the waterhole she rushed forward, gathered the sleeping child in her arms, and fled to her camp.

When Koromarange came back and saw that her granddaughter was missing, she knew what had happened. With eyes flashing with rage she crept

silently to her sister's camp. Knowing how sharp Prupe's ears had become she dared not make a sound. Breathing softly and controlling her anger, she watched her sister tie the child to a tree and leave the camp to get vegetables as a relish for the tasty meal she expected to enjoy that evening. As soon as Prupe was out of earshot Koromarange rushed into the camp and dug a hole in the ground. She put sharpened stakes at the bottom and covered the hole with branches of trees with soil packed tightly on top. Last of all she released Koakangi and took her back to her parents who by this time had returned from their hunting trip.

It was late afternoon before Prupe drew near the camp, a broad grin on her sunken mouth, with long runnels of saliva dripping from her chin as she thought of the succulent food she would soon be cooking. She caught her foot and stumbled, and with a cry of fear she crashed through the covering of soil and the scattered branches that hid the pit. For a few moments she clung desperately to the edge, scrabbling for a foothold and scattering the branches in every direction. Some of them fell in the fire and flared up, setting the scrub aflame. She raised one hand to shield her face from the fiery heat and fell headlong to the bottom of the pit where she was impaled on the sharp stakes.

If we were to go to Prupe's ancient camp we would find, even today, a vast pit thirty feet deep, surrounded by burnt and blackened vegetation, to remind us of the sorry end of Prupe the cannibal.

THE CASE OF THE MOTH

A QUEENSLAND hunter went on a long journey, taking his small son with him. It was hard for the little boy to keep up with his father, and day by day he grew thinner and weaker. Then came the rains. They fell without stopping until rivers rose and the land became one vast swamp. The little boy became ill. The only thing his father could do was to build a rough shelter of bark and branches of trees to keep the rain off him. Their food supplies had long been exhausted, and the man knew that his son would die if he was not given nourishing food quickly.

He tucked the boy up in his kangaroo-skin rug and splashed through the marsh in search of game. It was not easy to find in the flooded land, but after several days he found an opossum and killed it with his spear. He hurried back to the gunyah he had built, fearful that he might find his son lying there dead from starvation.

He arrived at the clearing, which he recognized by the broken branches of trees and the little mound that rose above the water, but of the gunyah and of his son there was no sign. He could not understand what had happened. He had been prepared to find his son's body, but the last thing he imagined was that it, and the little gunyah that sheltered it, would have disappeared as though by magic.

He leaned against a tree. His hand came in contact with a loose knob of bark and twigs on the trunk. He looked at it idly and then, with a sudden sense of shock, more closely, for it was a replica of the little gunyah he had built to shelter his son. He opened it with trembling fingers. Inside the case lay the white body of a grub, and he knew that the spirits had taken pity on the boy and saved him from death.

To this day the grub of the Case-moth always has a gunyah which it builds to protect it, and remind it of how, long ago, a father cared enough for his son to build a shelter for him while he sought for food.

THE COMING OF DEATH

THE first man ever to live in Australia was Ber-rook-boorn. He had been made by Baiame. After establishing Ber-rook-boorn and his wife in a place that was good to live in, he put his sacred mark on a yarran tree nearby, which was the home of a swarm of bees.

"This is my tree," he told them, "and these are my bees. You can take food anywhere you like in the land I have given you, but this tree, the bees, and the honey they make, you must never touch. If you do, much evil will befall you and all the people who will come after you."

He disappeared, and after he had gone, the first man and woman obeyed his instructions. But one day, when the woman was gathering firewood, her search carried her to Baiame's tree. The ground was littered with fallen branches. When she looked up and saw the sacred tree towering above her, she was terrified, but the easily gathered wood was so tempting that she came closer to gather an armful.

A brooding presence seemed to hover above her, and she raised her eyes once more. Now that she was closer to the tree she saw the bees hovering round the trunk, and drops of honey glittering on the bark.

She stared at them, fascinated by the sight. She had tasted the sweet excretion only once before, but here was food for many meals. She could not resist the lure of the shining drops. Letting her sticks fall to the ground, she began to climb the tree.

Suddenly there was a rush of air and a dark shape with huge black wings enveloped her. It was Narahdarn the Bat, whom Baiame had put there to guard his yarran tree. Ber-rook-boorn's wife scrambled down and rushed to her gunyah, where she hid in the darkest corner.

The evil she had done could never be remedied. She had released Narahdarn into the world, and from that day onwards he became the symbol of the death that afflicts all the descendants of Ber-rook-boorn.

It was the end of the golden age for Ber-rook-boorn and his wife, and the yarran tree wept bitterly at the thought. The tears coursed down the bark and solidified in the form of red gum which can often be found on yarran trees.

THE COMING OF SPRING

WILD, shrieking winds blow through the trees, stripping the leaves, and bending the tops until they are curved like boomerangs. Birds take shelter from the icy blast. Insects burrow into the ground. Animals huddle into any shelter they can find. In some places snow lies white on the ground. Even man must live on the food he has stored up and, while wind and rain turn the world into a place of desolation, he crouches on his tiny shelter made of bark or branches of trees.

It is winter.

The winds stop blowing one day, and all the living things hear a single, rolling peal of thunder. It is a sign that Mayra, the Spirit of Spring, has left her home and is coming closer, melting the snow and ice, touching the trees and plants with warm fingers.

Mayra is golden. Wattle trees burst into flower, and everywhere there are living clouds of green and yellow, and the many hues of the rainbow, as trees and plants rejoice in the presence of the gentle spirit.

The air is full of the music of waking birds; the very earth becomes a carpet of glowing colour; insects peer cautiously from their hiding places. When they see the goddess they rush into the sunshine and spread their wings, or uncoil their bodies from the long sleep. Animals are full of this new-found joy, and in men and animals the blood races in the veins, and happiness returns to the earth.

"If only it would be spring for ever," someone sighs, but Mayra knows that she is welcome only because she has chased away the spirits of gloom. She knows that eternal spring would become wearying. After the first rush of joy, she watches the sun as it grows in strength. When the heat of summer becomes almost unbearable, she knows it is time to be on her way.

But next year the Spirit of Spring will be back, and men and animals await her return with unwearied hope and joy.

DINGO AND NATIVE CAT

WHILE searching for food Dingo met Native Cat. They circled each other warily, each showing a bold front, yet secretly a little afraid of what the other might do. Dingo could not take his eyes off the other's sharp claws, while Native Cat looked uneasily at Dingo's strong white teeth.

The sun rose high and the men sought the shade of a banyan tree, taking care to keep well away from each other.

"Where do you come from?" Dingo asked. He had jerked into wakefulness and was fearful lest he should go to sleep again. It seemed better to spend his time talking rather than run the risk of putting himself at Cat's mercy.

"I live amongst the trees. I often see you running about on the plain. What a pity you can't climb."

"I don't have to sneak up into the trees to hide," Dingo said scornfully. "I'm able to look after myself."

"I don't hide either," Cat retorted. "It's cool here and, there's plenty of honey if you know where to look for it. But don't let's quarrel. It's too hot."

"I'm not quarrelling. And I'm not frightened of you either. I'm stronger than you."

Native Cat laughed.

"You may be stronger, but strength is not as important as you think. Anyone who can come back to life after he is dead fears no one."

23

"And who is able to come back to earth once his spirit has left his body?"

"I am."

"You!"

His tone was so sceptical that Cat jumped to his feet and said, "If you don't believe me, I will show you. Take your knife and cut off my head."

He knelt down and rested his neck on a log. Dingo took his knife from his belt and drove it into Cat's neck. The blood spurted from the jugular vein, but Dingo took no notice and hacked away until the head rolled across the sand and the body collapsed on the other side of the log.

"That's the end of you, Cat!" he said, and swaggered away.

Three days went by. Dingo built up his fire and lay down behind the brush shelter he had built. He was on the edge of sleep when he started up, every nerve alert. A voice came out of the darkness.

"Are you there, Dingo?"

"Who is it? Who is there?"

The voice spoke again, sounding thin and remote as though it was coming from the stars.

"I am Cat. I said I would come back. Here I am."

A bright glow shone in the sky. It moved and came closer. Native Cat jumped lightly to the ground and stood in front of Dingo, who was trembling from head to foot.

"Don't be afraid. All you have to do is to believe that you will come back. Let me show you."

He pushed Dingo down, and with a swift movement severed his head from his body.

"A pity he didn't have time to believe!" he said as he scooped a hole in the ground and buried Dingo's head.

It was Native Cat who taught men to bury their dead, and gave them the hope of reincarnation; but Dingo knows nothing of this. He became an animal destined to live out his days hunting in the arid desert lands, lacking the confidence he had when a man, having no hope of return to earth after he is dead.

THE DOGS THAT WERE REALLY SNAKES

BAHLOO, the moon god, waited until everyone was asleep before taking his three dogs for a walk. Bahloo was a friendly fellow, greatly liked by all the blackfellows; but the same

24

could not be said of his dogs. That was why he usually chose the hours of darkness to exercise them.

Sometimes Bahloo shows himself in the daytime. We have all seen his round, shining face sailing across the afternoon sky. It was on one such day that Bahloo was leading his dogs through the scrub when he came to a broad stream. A party of men was camped on the bank.

"A very pleasant day," Bahloo observed. They all smiled when they saw his round face.

"Well met, Bahloo," they shouted. "Why have you come here?"

"I am taking my dogs for a walk, but now I want to cross to the other side of the river. Will you carry them across for me?"

"No," they cried in unison. "No, we will not touch your dogs, Bahloo."

"Why is that?" asked the Moon.

No one answered him.

"Oh, come! If you will not help me, you must tell me why."

One, braver than the others, spoke for all of them.

"Bahloo, we all admire you. We would do anything for you—anything except come near your dogs. They do not harm you, but if we touched them they would kill us."

Bahloo was annoyed.

"I have made a simple request," he said, "and you have refused it. Look!"

He picked a piece of bark from the trunk of a tree and threw it in the river. It sank, and then bobbed up to the surface.

"You have seen the bark? If you do as I ask you, you will be like that piece of bark when you die. You will come back to life on earth again, just as I die and live again in my home in the sky. But if you disobey—watch again!"

He threw a stone into the water.

There was no need for him to say any more, for his meaning was clear to everyone.

"Oh, Bahloo, we love you, and we fear you, but we fear your dogs even more. They are not really dogs. They are snakes—the tiger snake, the death adder, and the black snake. Each one has poison fangs—we dare not touch them."

"Then when you die you will remain dead. Your bodies

will lose their flesh, and in the end your bones will crumble into dust."

With these words ringing in their ears, he picked up his snakes, which he called his dogs, wrapped them round his neck with their tails drooping over his shoulders and coiled round his arms, and waded through the water.

After that day Bahloo never talked with the people of earth again, but vindictively sent his "dogs" to plague them. Wherever they were, men killed them, but it was no use, for Bahloo was always watching, sending others to remind them of his dreadful words about death.

THE DUGONG, THE COCKATOOS, AND THE CHICKEN HAWK

Dugong and her brothers the Cockatoos were camped at the mouth of the river where food was plentiful. It was nearly midday and the heat waves were dancing above the hot sand. Dugong lay fast asleep among the rushes while her brothers went off on a hunting expedition.

"She will be quite safe here," they said. "No one can see her."

They did not know that Chicken Hawk was on the far side of the swamp. He was a lazy man.

"If I set fire to the rushes they will burn nicely on a day like this," he thought. "Then I will be able to get my food more easily."

He twirled his fire stick vigorously, and soon a wisp of smoke rose in the still air. The tinder glowed and the dry grass he had packed round it caught fire. The flames swept

across the lagoon. Chicken Hawk waded across as soon as they had died down and stumbled over the body of Dugong. He looked at the burnt flesh, recognised the young woman, and ran away quickly with fear in his heart, because he knew that her brothers the Cockatoos were famous fighting men.

Meanwhile they had seen the sudden flight of birds above the swamp, and the pall of smoke that hung over it.

"Our sister!" they cried, and ran along the beach and up to the swamp. The charred ends of the reeds were crumbling to ash and dropping into the water. They searched among them until they found their sister's body and lifted her tenderly in their arms. She stirred slightly and her eyelids fluttered.

"Who did it?" they asked. "Who tried to kill you and burn our homes?"

She could not speak. They laid her in a warm pool of water.

"Lie there, little sister. The water will heal your burns. We will find the man who has done this. He will never try to light a fire again when we have finished with him!"

They waded through the swamp and picked up Chicken Hawk's trail on the far side.

"It is Kalalang the Chicken Hawk!" they cried.

The trail led them inland across a bare stony plain where they could keep the trail in sight only because they were skilled huntsmen, and down to the beach. Chicken Hawk had waded through a stream and had climbed a tree, but the eagle-eyed hunters soon found him. They dragged him down and beat him with their spears until he was bruised and bleeding in a hundred places.

"Let me go!" he called feebly. "I am dying already. I did not mean to hurt your sister. I did not know she was lying among the reeds."

"We've punished him enough," one of the Cockatoos said. "He will never come back to our camping place by the shore again."

Chicken Hawk dragged himself painfully into the scrub and made his way inland, never daring to go down to the shore again. The Cockatoos went back to find their sister, but she had gone. She had had enough of men. She had swum out of the swamp and down the river to the sea, which she has discovered is a much better place for dugongs than the land.

WEEDAH the Mocking Bird was true to his name. He could imitate the voices of men and women, of crying babies, barking dogs, wind in the trees, the crackling of fire, and the running of water. Unfortunately he turned his talents to wicked purposes. He left the company of his fellow tribesmen and constructed a new encampment which contained many gunyahs.

Mocking Bird danced in and out of the tiny huts trying out his voice. One of the men who lived in the old camp was curious, and hid behind a tree. As he listened he heard many sounds—girls chattering together, children shouting as they raced round the camp, old men and women talking, someone singing, and all the other noises that come from a busy community, but there was no sign of life anywhere, except that a huge fire was burning in a cleared space. Wonderingly he tiptoed forward, stealing between the huts and peering through the doorways.

Weedah came out of one of the gunyahs and stood watching him with a smile on his face.

"Are you looking for someone?"

The man whirled round.

"Oh, it's you, Weedah! Where are all the others?"

"What others?"

"I heard the sound of many people, but your camp seems deserted now."

Weedah laughed and came towards him. The man stepped backwards. Weedah kept on walking, and the man retreated steadily before him until he felt the heat of the fire on his back.

"Stop! Stop!" he shouted. "You are mad, Weedah!"

Mocking Bird spread his arms and shrugged his shoulders.

"What is the matter with you, friend? No one invited you to my camp. I am lonely here, but some day men and women may come and fill the place with songs and laughter and talk. But they have not come yet. You are imagining things."

"I did hear them, Weedah." He shivered. "There is something strange about this place. I am going home."

Weedah stood in his way. As the man tried to edge round him, Mocking Bird lunged forward and sent him spinning into the fire.

A weird torrent of laughter swept through the camp as though many kookaburras were chattering together, but it was only Weedah laughing at his success.

As the days passed by Mocking Bird attracted many men and women into his camp by the magic of his voice, and burnt their bodies in the fire which was always kept alight. No one except the victims knew what had happened, but the suspicions of Mullian, the Eagle-hawk, had been roused. He scouted round and found that although many trails led to Weedah's encampment,

there were none coming from it except those of Mocking Bird himself.

Mullian, proud, self-reliant, and cunning, then knew what had happened to some of his closest friends. He decided that the time had come for Weedah to pay for his misdeeds. He stepped boldly out of the shelter of the trees and listened to the medley of sounds that came from the gunyahs. Weedah had become over-confident. When Eagle-hawk wandered amongst the shelters, he came up to him, asking the usual questions, and driving Mullian slowly towards the fire.

The crucial moment arrived. He launched himself at the larger man, but Mullian stepped aside, and as Weedah stumbled forward, he tripped him up. Mocking Bird tried to save himself. As he balanced precariously on his toes, Mullian took him in both hands, lifted him into the air, and hurled him into the fire. Mocking Bird's head struck heavily against a stone, and he lay still with the fire licking his clothes.

As Mullian was leaving the camp the air was rent by a violent explosion. The back of

Weedah's head broke in two, and from it came a bird which flew into the trees and began to chatter like a kookaburra, mocking the Eagle-hawk.

Weedah the Mocking Bird retained all the traits of Weedah the man who preyed on his own friends. Weedah the Mocking Bird still builds little shelters of grass, and imitates all the sounds of nature as he runs between the gunyahs.

A FIGHT WITH A KURREA

On the edge of the lagoon Toolalla was poised like a carved statue staring across the marshy waste. The Kurrea of the Boobera lagoon had terrorised the people who depended on the wild life of swamp and lake for their food, and they had appealed to Toolalla, who was a renowned warrior and hunter, to put an end to the monster. If the Kurrea had confined his attentions to ducks, swans, and fish, the tribespeople could have tolerated him, but no man dared paddle his canoe on the lagoon, nor even fish from the bank, because the Kurrea had developed a taste for human flesh. Sometimes he had even left the shelter of the quiet waters and had ploughed long furrows through the soil in his search for tasty morsels of human flesh.

Toolalla strained his eyes as he peered through the early morning mists. There was a ripple on the oily water, and quietly and menacingly a vast bulk emerged from a deep hole. Its eyes glared balefully at the hunter. Toolalla's arm went back, the woomera jerked forwards and his spear hurtled through the air, struck the Kurrea, and bounced off his skin, falling into the water

with a splash. Time after time Toolalla hurled his spears until none were left. The Kurrea swam through the reeds at the edge of the lagoon and charged up the bank, his mouth wide open, his fangs flickering between his teeth.

The hunter did not linger. The dust spurted from his heels as he raced through the scrub. He had no hope of escaping, but was determined to run until he dropped. The Kurrea gained on him quickly. His body was partly submerged in the ground, and the soil piled up against his breast like the bow wave of a canoe.

Toolalla veered to the left. In the distance he had caught sight of a bumble tree, and he wondered whether he could reach it before he was caught by the Kurrea. The bumble tree was the mother-in-law of the Kurrea and was the only living thing he feared. The hunter reached the tree and clung to it. The monster skidded to a halt and turned round in panic when he saw his mother-in-law. A deep hole was formed by the movement. Then the Kurrea raced back through the channel he had made in his pursuit of Toolalla.

The experience was a salutary one. He still needed food, and he preyed on the animal life of the lagoon, but no longer did he seize men. In fact the appearance of a canoe was enough to send him scurrying back to the bottomless hole where he had made his home. The channels he had made in the land in search of human victims, including the one that had been formed during his final excursion in pursuit of Toolalla, were filled with water in the rainy season, but at other times they were quite dry.

The Kurrea no longer haunts the lagoon, but his descendants are the Gowarkees, the giant emus with black feathers and red legs which live in the swampy country near the home of Baiame.

THE FIRST BULLROARER

WHILE the Byama brothers were hunting they left their young sons, who had both been named Weerooimbrall, on a small plateau surrounded by large rocks. They thought the boys would be safe in this sheltered spot, but they had reckoned without Thoorkook and his dogs. They had offended Thoorkook some time before, and at last the chance for revenge had arrived. He had seen the two brothers climbing up the hill behind their camp, accompanied by their sons, and had watched them leave the plateau without them. His dogs raced through the scrub and up the hillside, and by the time Thoorkook gained the rocky shelf, he found them fighting over the remains of the two mangled bodies.

.   .   .   .

All night long the dismal chanting went on in the Byama camp as the boys' relatives mourned their loss. At sunrise the fathers were intent on revenge, but nothing could assuage the grief of the two mothers. They went about the day's work quietly with the tears rolling down their cheeks and hissing into the cooking fire. When night came their cries broke out again. They wandered away from the camp. The other members of the tribe shivered and went inside their wurleys, blocking their ears against the mournful sound. Night after night it continued until at last the women were changed into curlews, whose wailing will continue through the long nights until the end of time.

"We have lost our sons," the elder Byama said, "and now our wives have gone too. We are not men if we do not kill Thoorkook and his dogs."

"It is true," his brother agreed, "but Thoorkook is a bad man and his dogs will tear us to pieces if we go into his camp."

"Many dogs, much fear, brother. One dog, little fear."

Byama the younger understood. "But how?" he asked.

"I will show you."

He tied a rolled up skin to his girdle and began the slow rhythm of the kangaroo dance. He shouted and muttered spells, and gradually his arms shrivelled, his legs grew thick and strong, and the skin roll changed into a tail. The man was gone and in his place stood a kangaroo. Byama the younger wondered what his brother was going to do, but he followed his example, and presently two large kangaroos hopped towards Thoorkook's encampment.

The dogs scented them and came towards them snarling, straining to reach them. The kangaroos bounded away with the dogs hot in pursuit. One, stronger and swifter than the others, got well ahead of the rest of the pack. When it was close to their heels the kangaroos stopped and swung their tails at it until its head was pounded to pulp. The other dogs had nearly reached them by the time they had finished. Away they went once more until another dog took the lead.

All through the day the kangaroo brothers bounded round the plain, waiting until a single dog came close enough for them to deal with it. By the end of the day every dog had been killed. The brothers changed back to human form, stalked into the camp of the killer of their sons, and slowly and deliberately put him to death. Thoorkook's spirit took flight and became a solitary mopoke.

The shame of the death of the Weerooimbralls was over, but the killing of Thoorkook could not restore the boys to life nor bring back the curlew wives, and the brothers were lonely men.

One day Byama the younger was using his axe to prise a grub from a crevice in a tree trunk when he dislodged a large piece of bark. It hurtled through the air, spinning so quickly that it made a peculiar sound. The elder brother turned round.

"It is the voice of my son!" he whispered.

He concealed his excitement. "There's no game here," he said to his brother. "You go over there and I will go in the opposite direction. We will meet in camp tonight."

As soon as the younger Byama was out of sight he dropped to his knees and examined the chip, turning it over in his hands, wondering how he could make it spin through the air as it had done when it had sprung from the tree trunk. He threw it up many times, but it fell to the ground without a sound. He took out his knife, cut a small hole in one end of the chip, tied it to a long piece of string which he took from his bag, and whirled it round his head. Again the soft voice of the Weerooimbrall was heard.

Taking his stone axe with him, Byama went back to the tree and cut a much larger piece of thin wood. He fashioned it to the same shape as the piece of bark, bored a hole at the end, tied it to a strong cord, and whirled it round his head.

Byama the younger was on his way home, burdened with the day's catch. He rushed up to his brother.

"I have heard the voice of my son Weerooimbrall!" he shouted.

"He is not here. You know he is dead."

"But I heard him. His voice was loud and clear."

"Was it like this?"

The elder Byama swung the thin piece of wood at the end of the cord.

It whirled and twirled and cried like a human voice.

"What is it?" the younger Byama asked in a bewildered manner. "What are you doing? It is my son speaking and calling to me!"

"No, brother, it is not your son. It is not my son. But their spirits live in this piece of wood, crying to us with their own voices."

And so the first bullroarer was made. It was a sacred thing that preserved the spirits of the boys who had been killed by Thoorkook. It was never shown to women. It needed only to be swung on a string to bring the boys' voices to life.

As the years went by it entered into the initiation rites of young men, who were told that the spirits of the Weerooimbralls were present, sharing the experiences of manhood with them, preserving them from evil, and strengthening them in their ordeal.

THE FIRST MAN IN THE SOUTHERN CROSS

BAIAME once travelled far across the land he had made, and was lonely because there was no one to talk with. He scraped red earth up in his hands and fashioned it into the shape of human beings. Two men he made, and then there was only enough earth left to make a single woman. It was asking for trouble, but Baiame did not know enough about the children of his creation to realise this. He lived with them,

teaching them what plants were good to eat, how to dig roots from the ground, and where the best grubs were to be found.

"With these, and water to drink, you can live, and your bellies will never be empty," he said.

After that he left them, and returned to his home in the sky. For some time the three people lived happily together, but after a while there came a long and severe drought. The plants withered, roots were difficult to find, and the grubs seemed to have disappeared.

"We must find something to eat, or we will starve," the woman said.

"But there is nothing left."

"There are animals. We must hunt them, and then there will be flesh to eat and blood to drink."

The men looked at her in consternation.

"The Father Spirit has not given us permission to kill the animals he made," they objected.

"But he didn't say we were not to kill them," she replied. "I am sure he expects us to think for ourselves."

One of the men was convinced. He stalked a small kangaroo and killed it with a sharp stone.

"Now what will we do?" he asked.

"I will show you," the woman said.

She dug a shallow hole and burnt wood in it till a glowing heap of embers and hot stones lay at the bottom. She singed the fur of the kangaroo and roasted the flesh.

"There we are," she said. "Let us fill our bellies with the good food that Baiame has provided."

The hunter squatted down beside her, and they sank their teeth in the half-cooked meat.

"It is good!" the man said, his eyes alight with appreciation. "Come and taste the new food," he called to his companion.

The other man moved away.

"This is not what Baiame taught us. A dreadful thing will happen because you have done this thing. I would rather starve than eat one of Baiame's children."

Nothing they could say would make him change his mind. The smell of roasted flesh nauseated him, and he ran across the plain. The others followed him at a distance. He was faint with hunger, and presently he fell at the foot of a white gum tree and lay still.

The others looked at him in astonishment which changed to fear when a dark spirit with flashing eyes dropped down from the branches of the tree. It picked up the body of their friend and threw it so that it fell into the trunk of a hollow tree. Then it sprang after the body. Two white cockatoos, disturbed by the movements of the evil spirit, screeched and fluttered round in circles.

The tree groaned, the soil was disturbed as the roots were jerked out of the ground. It rose up in the air, followed by the cockatoos, and dwindled in the infinite space of the sky. Darkness fell, and nothing could be seen but the white specks that were the cockatoos, and four fiery eyes which glared out of the hollow trunk. They were the eyes of their friend and the evil spirit.

The tree was lost to sight, but the four points of light, which were the eyes of the man and the spirit, and the white wings of the cockatoos mounted up into the sky. The eyes remained inside the white gum tree which is known as Yaraan-do, and became the stars of the constellation of the Southern Cross, while the white cockatoos, which followed them, are the Pointers.

FISH HAWK AND LYREBIRD

The pool lay dark and still in the shadow of the trees. Fish Hawk was just as still as the pool, lying on his back with his legs stretched out, fast asleep. He had spent the morning crushing poisonous berries. When he had finished he poured the juice into the pool and went to sleep knowing that when he woke the fish would be dead and floating on the surface. He smiled in his sleep and dreamed of the big feed he would soon be having.

He did not wake up, even when Lyrebird came out of the bush and began to spear the fish. The poison had not had time to take effect, but before long the newcomer had a good supply. He lit a fire and began

to roast them. Fish Hawk woke with a start and realised that Lyrebird had deliberately taken

advantage of him. He stole up behind him, quietly gathered up the spears which Lyrebird had put by his side, and retreated to the shelter of the trees. He chose the tallest tree he could find, climbed to the top, and lashed the spears to the trunk. Back on the ground, he looked up and admired his work. The spears looked like a feathery branch at the top of the tree. He hid under a bush and waited to see what would happen.

Lyrebird made a leisurely meal and then put out his hand to gather up his spears. His groping fingers failed to find them. He searched everywhere with a puzzled expression, but there was no other place where he could have left them. Fish Hawk laughed silently as he watched from his hiding place and saw Lyrebird running round and round the pool, looking everywhere for the missing spears. It was even funnier when he began to talk to himself.

"Someone has been here while I was cooking fish," Lyrebird said aloud. "Who could it be? What would he do with them? He could bury them, but there is no sign of the soil being disturbed. He could run away with them, of course, but then I would see the marks of his flight through the bush. And he could hide them in a tree."

He walked through the bush, looking up and down the trees until at last he saw the spears waving in the breeze. Lyrebird was a man who did not believe in working when there was an easier way to do things. He called on the spirits of water, and streams, and floods, and at his word the water in the pool rose quickly and carried him on its surface to the top of the tree, where he retrieved the spears, sinking down to the ground as the water receded.

Poor Fish Hawk was caught in the flood and swept out to sea. He has never been able to get back to his quiet pool again, but lives on the sea coast.

Lyrebird never forgot his experience that day. Everywhere he goes he searches the tree tops for his spears.

FISH MOON

THE sisters swam across the channel that divided the island from the mainland and pulled themselves up the rocky shore. It was not a large island but many trees grew there, and there was an open grassy space which contained a tiny lake, where the water glistened with the changing colours of an opal.

"This is a good place to be," one of the women said. "I would like to live here for ever. Just think, no babies to feed, no food to cook, water to drink right at our feet, grass growing on the hot ground, and shady trees to shelter us from the sun."

"And no one to bother us," her sister replied, throwing herself on the grassy carpet and stretching luxuriously. "Wonderful! But we couldn't live here for ever."

"Why not?"

"Why not? Don't be silly. We would miss the men after a while. It wouldn't really be exciting, would it?"

"Excitement! Who wants excitement all the time? Much better to rest and eat, sleep and play, whenever we feel like it."

"But what about food? What could we live on?"

"Roots and shellfish and grubs. Probably there are yams somewhere, and there must be water-lily roots in the lake . . ."

She sat up and pointed excitedly. ". . . and fish! Look!"

The rounded back of a large fish curved out of the water and slid out of sight. The woman jumped up and ran round the edge of the lake to a place where a rock hung over the water. She lay flat on her belly, the fingers of one hand clutching the edge of the rock. In the other hand she held a spear, point down, ready to strike. The fish swam unsuspectingly below the rock. There was a flurry in the water as the spear flashed in the sunlight and pierced its body.

"Quick, sister, come and help me!"

They jumped into the lake, caught the dying fish in their hands, and threw it on to the bank.

"There!" gasped the woman who had speared it. "I told you there was plenty of food. It's as easy as that. You can gather a big pile of firewood while I find a place to make an oven."

The fire was soon crackling merrily, and before long the sand and stones were hot enough to bake the fish.

"Doesn't it smell good?"

"Yes, maybe," the other said grudgingly, "but fish is not much good by itself. We need roots and all sorts of vegetable food."

"What an aggravating

woman you are ... never satisfied with anything. I tell you this island has everything we want. Take your digging stick and see what you can find over there. I'll go in the other direction. You see, we'll soon have as much as we can eat. Don't forget to take your dilly bag with you. You'll need it."

Much later they returned, their bags well filled, their mouths watering at the thought of the feast that was in store for them. They made their way to where the column of smoke was rising lazily in the still evening air, and looked down at the fire in astonishment. The stones shimmered with the heat, but the fish was gone.

They could see where it had dragged itself out of the soft sand and across the grass to the shelter of the trees. They followed its trail without difficulty and tracked it to the foot of a tall tree.

"Look!"

The fish was half-way up the trunk, climbing steadily upwards. The woman who had speared it caught the lowest branch and began to climb the tree but her sister clung on to her and said, "Don't be foolish. You might fall and injure yourself. Where can the fish go?

When it reaches the small branches at the top it will probably fall, and we can put it back on the fire."

They watched the fish growing smaller as it inched its way up the trunk. The top swayed to and fro when it reached the uppermost twigs, but the fish did not stop. It floated upwards where the black mantle of night and the twinkling stars had veiled the blue sky. By now the fish had swelled until it was perfectly round. Its skin was silver and shining with a steady light. The women watched it for hours until it drifted away and sank behind the hills of the mainland.

Two puzzled women lay close to the fire that night. When morning came they cooked the vegetables they had gathered, and roasted cockles in the embers of the fire. They could hardly wait for night to come to see if the fish would appear in the sky. The sun went down, and they knew that the fish was coming long before they saw it, because a radiance was streaming across the eastern sky. It rose slowly and majestically, but it was a little smaller than it had been when it climbed the tree and escaped from the earth. It was no longer round but slightly flattened as though it had been lying on its side.

Every night the sky was clear. Every night the fish made its long journey from east to west. Every night it grew smaller until, after many nights, it was only a thin, curved sliver of light ... and then it was gone, and everything was dark. The island seemed a pleasant place no longer. As soon as morning came the sisters swam back to their own home, to the husbands they had deserted, and to the unending work that is the lot of those who bear children.

There came an evening when the fish appeared again in the east. Every night it grew larger until it was perfectly round. Then something began to eat it away, but it grew once more, and dwindled, and grew, as it has been doing ever since.

THE FLIES AND THE BEES

FLIES are troublesome, improvident insects who present a great contrast to the Bees, who store up food for winter and are always busy providing for the future. Their ancestors the Bunnyyarl and the Wurrunnunnah were just the same. The two tribes lived together, but they had little in common.

Throughout the hot summer days the Wurrunnunnah were kept busy making galleries and storerooms for their children, and to hold the delicious honey they gathered from the flowers. It was an endless task, and they were exasperated at the improvidence of the Bunnyyarl, who had no thought for the severity of the coming winter, and who seemed to delight in poking about

amongst the filth of their scattered home, seeking for food which they ate as soon as they found it.

"You will be sorry when winter comes," they were told. "It will be no use coming to beg for food from us."

"We won't come to you," buzzed the flies. "We don't like your honey, and we don't like you. Leave us alone."

When the nights began to grow longer, the Bunnyyarl romped gaily round the camp, but the Wurrunnunnah noticed that when no one seemed to be looking, they raided the Ant food stores. They held a meeting in the galleries of their home.

"The Bunnyyarl have no food stored up yet," one of them said. "When the cold winds of winter blow across the plains they will starve to death."

"I think not," said an old man. "They have not heeded our warnings, but they will expect us to feed them."

"To feed thousands and thousands of Bunnyyarls!" someone exclaimed. "We'd have nothing left for ourselves.

We had better leave them, and be quick about it."

Every one agreed. The Wurrunnunnahs turned into Bees, and in the twilight they flew away to a distant place, where they chose secure hiding places in hollow trees. They worked from early morning till late at night, building the wax galleries, filling them with honey, gathering their winter food into wax vessels which filled every corridor. When winter finally came, they sealed the entrances to their villages and spent the long months drowsily eating and waiting for spring to wake them up to work once more.

The Bunnyyarl were dismayed when they found that the Wurrunnunnah had deserted them. They crawled into holes and crevices in the rocks and bark of trees, but the icy fingers of winter followed them and shrivelled up their bodies. So it is that flies die in the winter, says the blackfellow, but because the ways of Baiame are past understanding, he creates myriads of new flies to annoy mankind every summer.

Of all the Bandicoots who lived in the long, infertile valley there was none to compare with Bilba. She was three times the size of a normal Bandicoot. Her paws were broad and strong. When she began to dig in the dry soil it was as though Wurrawilberoo himself had descended in a whirling sandstorm.

There were no natural enemies of the Bandicoot tribe in the valley. It offered little food or shelter for other animals, and worst of all, there was no water to drink except at the bottom of the deep holes dug by the Bandicoots.

One day the silence was broken by the sharp voices of the Dingoes who had been driven away from their own hunting grounds by a severe drought. With ears pricked, tense and suspicious, they came over the ridge, sniffing the breeze and peering about with hungry glances.

"Look!" the leader exclaimed. "Bandicoots!"

They rushed down the slope. The leader caught sight of Bilba and turned sharply.

"Follow me," he barked. "See that enormous Bandicoot

down there by the tree? There will be a fine meal for us tonight, brothers."

He was answered by yells of delight which startled Bilba. She lifted her head and stared at the pack which was almost upon her. Smothering a scream, she raced up the valley. With her powerful legs she was able to draw away from her pursuers. When the gap had grown wide enough she lowered her head and dug frantically with her paws. Within seconds she was lost to sight in a whirling cloud of dust. The leading

Dingo penetrated the storm of sand and discovered the hole in the ground.

"She has gone to earth," he shouted. "We must dig her out."

Although he knew he was no match for the giant Bandicoot, he had the support of his followers. They widened the hole until the broken burrow was lit by the sun's rays. Heaving herself up on her hind legs, Bilba sprang out, darted swiftly between the Dingoes, and continued uphill. Barking and snapping at her heels, the Dingoes strained every muscle in an attempt to leap on her back, but Bilba was too swift for them. She drew slowly ahead and burrowed once more into the ground. The Dingoes were relentless in their pursuit. Time after time they flushed Bilba from her hastily dug burrow. She reached the end of the valley, so bare and unattractive to others but so dear to her and all her friends, and dug her way frantically into the ground for the last time. While the Dingoes were widening the tunnel at one end she bored deeper and deeper into the ground. She felt moist sand under her paws and dug even

faster. The sand swirled madly in the confined space and in a moment she found herself standing up to her belly in muddy water. The ground stirred under her feet and a jet of clear water shot upwards. It carried Bilba with it and rolled her on the ground. The hole filled to the brim with water, the Dingoes were swept together in a bunch, bowled head over tail, thrown violently against each other, banged against the rocks that were embedded in the sand and, bruised and half drowned, the whole pack was washed ashore. They scrambled to their feet and raced out of the hostile valley as fast as their legs could carry them.

The spring of water did not dry up. It kept welling up in the hole that Bilba had dug, and soaked into the thirsty earth. It trickled down the valley, filling every hole to the brim, and running on to the next, until there was a chain of silver pools in the arid soil.

The Dingoes did not return. It is a long time since Bilba died, and there has never been another giant Bandicoot in the valley, but the water she brought from the depths of the earth has made it a flowering Paradise, a land of green grass and leafy trees and flowers that never stop blooming.

THE FROG AND THE FLIES

The Flies, man and wife, were tired of their camping ground which was known as the Place of Flies.

"Come along," said Fly husband. "Pack your dilly bag and we will see if we can find a better place than this."

"But where can we go?"

"Oh, come on," Fly said in the impatient manner of husbands. "I know where to go."

They had not travelled far before they were overtaken by Frog.

"Here comes our old friend Frog," Fly said, but Fly wife scowled and said nothing because she did not trust him.

They journeyed together in company for several days, sharing the same fire at night, gathering honey, and catching an occasional goanna or wallaby for meat, but leaving Fly wife to find grubs and roots. One evening they came to a place called Tatapikanam, the Place of Frogs.

"This is my permanent camp," Frog said proudly. "Make yourselves at home."

The following morning he lay back with his hands behind his head and said, "You will find plenty of honey over there."

"Where?"

"Oh, as far as you can see. There's a tree where the honey ants live. Bring back plenty and then you won't have to go back for a day or two."

"Aren't you coming with us?" asked Fly.

"No. I have a lot of work to do round the camp," Frog replied.

As soon as the husband and wife were out of sight he stretched himself luxuriously and went to sleep again.

When the Flies returned Frog was still asleep.

"I told you so," Fly wife hissed. "Now that he's got us here he'll make us work our fingers to the bone while he lives in idleness."

Frog woke up with a start and thanked them for the honey they had brought. Fly wife opened her mouth but her husband kicked her on the shin and she closed it again; but it was set in a firm line which presaged trouble for someone. It was not long before trouble came.

Early the next morning the Flies were woken by a hearty shout from Frog.

"Come on, come on," he boomed. "Time you were awake. I'm really hungry this morning, and after we've had something to eat there's a lot of work to be done."

"Then you can begin straight away," Fly wife snapped. "Take the honey and mix it with water."

"Oh, I can't do that," Frog protested. "It's too early in the morning. My hands are too cold."

"It's not too cold for me to get the meal ready, is it?"

Frog stood up and threw out his chest.

"Listen to me. This is my camp, and while you are here you will do as I tell you."

"Oh ho, that's it, is it?" Fly wife screamed. "I knew what was going to happen as soon as you joined us. Listen to me for a change. If you don't mix that honey at once there'll be nothing for you to eat today or any other day."

Frog lunged forward and struck her on the ear with his clenched fist. Up to this time Fly had been keeping discreetly in the background, but when his wife was attacked he was forced to come to her assistance. Fly and Frog struck each other. Frog tripped and fell on his face. Fly wife caught him by the hair and banged his face up and down on the stony ground. They rolled over and fell in a water hole. When Frog came to the surface Fly wife picked up a handful of mud and plastered it over his forehead. He scrambled out, picked up a charred stick from the remains of the fire and poked both the husband and wife in the eyes. They blundered about, clutching each other and trying to reach their enemy.

"I've had enough of Flies," Frog shouted. "It is my home, remember. Get out of here."

He jumped back into the water hole and croaked, "Braka, braka, braka."

There was a big, flattened lump on his forehead where Fly wife had plastered mud over him, and his eyes were big and protuberant.

"Glub, glub," he went, and sank out of sight in the pool called Tatapikanam, the Place where Frog was hit.

The Flies staggered down the bank of the stream, falling over and helping each other up again. They could hardly see and their faces were black with charcoal. They jumped into the stream, blinking their eyes to clear them.

"Let us stay here," Fly wife said. "This is a good place."

Her husband looked at her in astonishment. Her face and body were black, her eyes bulged from her head, she had thin legs—two, four, six of them—and gauzy wings.

"Don't look at me," she said. "You look the same as I do. This is now the home of Flies. If any man comes here we will fly into his eyes and make them swell up just as ours are swollen."

So it remains, Nonpannyinna, the Place of Flies.

THE FROG FOOD OF THE BUNYIP

Down in the billabong a head was concealed among the reeds. It remained so still that none of the wild creatures noticed it. Three ducks paddled past. In the darkness there was a sudden movement. Two hands shot out and seized their legs, pulling the ducks under water and twisting their necks so quickly and silently that the third duck drifted away without knowing what had happened to the others.

The Frog man stood up, shivering a little in the cool night breeze. He tied the ducks to his girdle and was about to wade ashore, where his wife was waiting for him, when he saw a vast grey shape loom out of the swamp. It was a Bunyip, the dreadful monster of marsh and billabong.

The young man did not waste his breath in shouting. He waded through the shallow water in frenzied haste towards the bank. His wife had also seen the Bunyip.

"Give me the ducks," she called as he came closer.

He handed them up to her, scrambled on to the bank, and lay down, panting for breath.

"There's no time to wait here," she said. "The monster is getting closer."

"Wait till I get my breath," he gasped.

"Come on," she urged him. "The Bunyip will get us if you don't hurry."

She pulled him to his feet, but as she did so the Bunyip stretched out his long arm, and his claws closed round her body. Her husband caught her by the arm and tried to save her, but the Bunyip lifted her up, tucked her under his arm, and disappeared into the darkness.

The man was desperate. He plunged into the water and waded through the rushes, but they had closed behind the monster, leaving no trace of his passage.

As soon as it was light next morning the Frog man gathered a supply of the little creatures who were his totem and tied them to a long pole which he stuck in the mud. They cried and croaked miserably, waving their arms and legs in a struggle to free themselves.

"That will fetch the Bunyip," the Frog man thought. He was crouching among the reeds with his war spear beside him, ready to thrust it into the Bunyip as soon as it appeared. The hours passed slowly. The only thing he could see was the wriggling of the frogs' legs. The daylight faded, and through the night the croaking of the frogs grew fainter. By morning they were all dead. Sadly he untied them, caught some more, and tied them to the pole. The air was filled with a fresh babel of sound as he went to his camp to sleep.

When he returned that night the frogs were gone, and the pole lay on its side among the reeds. With fresh hope he caught a further supply, erected the pole again, tied the frogs in place, and sat down to wait.

Morning after morning the Frog man baited his trap, but never once did he catch sight of the Bunyip. It was only when he could not keep his eyes open for lack of sleep that they were taken. But at length his patience was rewarded. It was early morning. The young husband was about to end his lonely vigil when a huge shape parted the veils of mist, and the Bunyip reached out his claws to take the frogs. Behind it the young woman followed with vacant eyes, dirty and unkempt, with her hair straggling down her face.

"Keep away," her husband shouted, and threw his spear at the monster. It sank into the soft flesh so that only the end of the handle was showing. The Bunyip groaned and threw the frogs at its aggressor. One of them hit the Frog man in the eye, blinding him for a moment. He still had his throwing stick. He hurled it at the Bunyip, and had the satisfaction of seeing it disappear into one of the Bunyip's eyes. The creature turned round, shrieking with pain, and blundered back the way it had come.

"Come to me, wife," the Frog man implored. "You will be safe with me."

To his astonishment the young woman took no notice but followed the Bunyip into the mist. Her husband ran after her. There was no mistaking the trail now. With only one eye, the Bunyip slipped and fell, picked itself up and staggered on leaving a trail of crushed vegetation behind it. The woman followed close at its heels, for the Bunyip had cast a spell over her which bound her closely to him.

They reached the far side of the billabong. The Bunyip heaved itself out of the water and began to climb a gum tree. It reached the top, sat on a branch, and glared down at the Frog man with its single baleful eye. The young woman stood at the foot of the tree as though petrified.

"You are safe now," her husband said, holding out his arms. "Come with me and we will return to our camp."

She put out her arms, but could not move her feet, which appeared to be frozen to the ground. He took a step towards her, and suddenly stood still. He had come within the circle of the power that bound his wife to the Bunyip, and was unable to move.

Day turned to night, night to day, rain storms swept across the billabong, the water rose and fell with the changing seasons, but still the little tableau remained by the gum tree. The petrified bodies of the Frog man and his wife stood like gaunt stumps of trees, with arms stretched out towards each other in longing, while far above them the single eye of the Bunyip glared from the leaves of the tree.

Then came a great storm which overthrew the gum tree. The eye remained where it was, but the spell was broken, and at last the couple were reunited. Their descendants will never touch the little frogs again. They leave them as food for the Bunyips so that the monsters of the swamp will not molest them.

And where the Murray River now flows, the blackfellows say that the moon is the eye of the Bunyip that once stole the wife of a Frog man of their tribe.

THE FROGS AT FLOOD TIME

BIRRA-NULU, the wife of Baiame, was the flood-sender. It may be that she was too engrossed in the love-play of the Father Spirit, or even that she was tired and lazy, but whatever may be the reason, she did not fill the streams with flood waters as regularly as men would wish.

When the streams died away to a tiny trickle of water, and the sun's rays poured from a cloudless sky all day, the wirrinuns, the medicine men, hurried to her home in the sky and made their complaints.

If Birra-nulu was in a good mood and saw fit to grant their request, she would send her messengers to tell the wirrinuns to warn the Frog people that a flood would soon be coming.

Then the messengers would scurry to and fro proclaiming, "Let the Bun-yun Bun-yuns hurry to the river. Call the Bun-yun Bun-yuns. Hurry up, every Bun-yun Bun-yun. You are needed at the river. The ball of blood is nearly here!"

The Frog people were strong, and able to lift heavy stones. When they heard the messengers calling to them they hurried to the stream, where fires had been lit along the banks. They rolled stones into the fires and sat beside them, looking up the dry bed of the stream expectantly, while the stones slowly turned red and white in the heat.

Meanwhile Birra-nulu had made the ball of blood, and one of her messengers had sent it rolling down the river bed. Presently it came in sight—a huge red sphere gleaming in the sunlight, reaching from bank to bank, and apparently growing quickly in size as it came towards them. The nearest

Bun-yun Bun-yuns sprang to their feet, caught the white-hot stones from the fire, tossed them from hand to hand, and threw them into the red ball. Like a bursting bubble it broke, and in a moment filled the stream from one bank to the other in a foaming torrent of blood.

As the red stream raced past, the Bun-yun Bun-yuns hurled the hot stones into it to purify it. The thick, repulsive liquid turned pale, and finally became crystal-clear water as it was refined by the stones. The Frog men kept on shouting, uttering cries of encouragement. Warned by their hoarse shouting, the tribesmen dashed over to the river and filled their coolamons with the refreshing water.

The Bun-yun Bun-yuns always warn the tribes when the floodwaters begin to rise. If

they are discoloured and red with mud and silt, it is said that the Frogs have been lazy and have not purified the water properly; but when they run clear, and sparkle in the sunlight, the Bun-yun Bun-yuns have done their work well.

THE FROG, THE WALLABY, AND THE DUGONG

Two young mothers went down to the beach to gather cockles, carrying their coolamons under their arms. In each coolamon was a tiny baby, laughing and waving its arms and legs in the air.

Moodja's baby was pretty

and had been greatly admired by the older women, but Mamanduru's baby was ugly. The women put the babies under a shady tree and were soon engaged in picking up shellfish and putting them in their baskets. The cockles were not very plentiful, and before long the two mothers had wandered some distance from the tree where the babies were lying.

Presently Mamanduru called, "My coolamon is full. Are you ready to come now?"

Moodja was surprised. "I haven't got many yet. You must have found a good patch of them. You can go if you want, and I'll follow later. Have a look at my baby as you go past and see if he's all right."

Mamanduru hurried back to the tree. She tipped the shellfish on the ground, picked up Moodja's baby, put it into the empty coolamon, and went into the bush with it. She concealed her tracks, being careful not to break any twigs that were lying on the ground, and avoiding patches of soft earth. When she came to a stream she climbed along an overhanging branch, dropped into the water, and waded upstream until she came to some smooth stones and baked clay that would leave no trace of her passage. Mamanduru ran back until she came to the sea, and was soon playing happily with the baby in the shelter of a clump of pandanus trees where she thought the other woman would never find her.

When Moodja had gathered a good supply of cockles, she went back to the tree. She heard a baby crying and quickened her steps. To her amazement the baby was not there, but only the ugly little child of Mamanduru. She realised that the jealous woman had stolen her baby, leaving her own offspring in his place. She picked the baby up in her arms and set out to follow its mother's trail.

Her face hardened as she bent low and peered at the ground. There were no footprints or broken twigs to tell her where to go, but her sharp eyes saw a tiny twig pressed into the ground, and a few ants crushed on the harder soil near by. It was a long, slow task, but at last she came to the stream and reasoned that the fugitive would have waded along its bed. There was no way to tell whether she should go up the stream or down, so she travelled downstream for some distance, but could not pick up any sign of the trail. When she came to the coast she searched the beach before turning inland, and saw an unexpected movement at a distance. She walked towards the group of trees and felt a surge of relief as she recognised Mamanduru. She stood in front of the woman, who was seated on the ground looking at the baby who was lying on its back and laughing.

Moodja's anger boiled over. She tossed the ugly, misshapen baby she was holding into the tree.

"What are you doing with my baby?" she demanded.

"It's not your baby. It's mine."

Moodja rushed up to Mamanduru, grabbed her by the hair, and jerked her to her feet.

"Give me my baby," she shouted.

When the ugly baby's mother made no reply, she shook her, still holding her by the hair. Mamanduru groped until she found her digging stick. Moodja reeled back from the pain of the blow she received on her head and fell over. Her hand closed over another stick, dusty and blackened by fire. She jabbed it into her opponent's eyes, bruising them and filling them with ashes and charred wood. The woman made one last blow at Moodja which broke her legs and sent her hopping off into the trees before she fell to the ground. The baby clung to Mamanduru's back even when she crawled on all fours to the water to try to wash the ashes from her eyes.

The ugly baby was changed into a frog with a big mouth; Moodja, hopping on her broken legs, turned into a wallaby; while Mamanduru waded far into the sea and swam away from the shore in the form of a dugong with tiny eyes, and with Moodja's baby clinging to her back.

THE GIFTS OF THE SUN GODDESS

WHEN all animals, insects, birds, and reptiles had the appearance of men, they were dissatisfied. They went to Yhi, the sun goddess, and begged her to give them the gifts they longed for. The goddess took pity on them.

"I will grant all your requests," she said, "but remember this. Once I have given you what you want you will never be able to change back to what you are now. Are you satisfied?"

"Yes, yes," they all cried.

52

"Give us our hearts' desire."

"Very well. Who is first?"

"I am," said Mouse.

"And what do you want, my little one?"

"I want wings to fly with."

The sun goddess waved her hand and long, leathery wings sprouted from Mouse's legs and arms until it was transformed into Bat that flies by night.

Seal lumbered up.

"I have had too much of the land," he said. "My body is far too heavy, and I hurt myself when I scrape between the trees."

Yhi smiled sympathetically at the unwieldy Seal.

"Here are flippers for you," she replied. "You will still be able to walk on land, but your real home will be in the cool waters of the sea, where you will be able to dive and swim like a fish."

"I'm next," said Owl.

"But you can fly. What more do you want?"

"I want bigger eyes, so that the other animals will admire me."

"There you are, Owl ... but perhaps you will be sorry some day for being vain."

Her words came true. Owl could no longer bear the light of day, and had to spend the daylight hours deep in the heart of the bush, coming out only at night when his large eyes could see in the darkness.

Last of all, after the other animals had had their wishes granted, Koala came prancing up to the sun goddess, waving his long, bushy tail from side to side, and exciting the envy of the others. Unfortunately Koala was not aware of their admiration.

"Take it away," he begged. "It is useless. Take it away!"

And Yhi took Koala's tail away, to his everlasting sorrow.

GOANNA AND HIS STRIPES

AGAIN it was in the days when animals walked on two legs and were in every way as human beings. There were two tribes which lived together, Mungoongali the Goannas, and Piggiebillah the Porcupines. It was an uneasy association, for their ancestors, who came from distant lands in the west, had been of different types. The Goannas were born thieves, while the Porcupines were a much more self-reliant tribe, and were expert hunters.

In the eastern plain to which

the two tribes had migrated, the Piggiebillahs occupied themselves in hunting, but the food of the Mungoongalis was confined to the sugar-bags of the honey ants, which they gathered by climbing trees, and to food which they stole from the stores of the Porcupines. It is sad to relate that their depredations went further than this, for the unprotected children of the Mungoongalis were killed and eaten in secret.

On one occasion the Goannas invited their neighbours to join them on a hunting expedition. The Porcupines laughed scornfully.

"Have you become expert in the chase since yesterday, or the day before?" they asked. "Thank you for your offer, but we will do much better without you."

"Please come with us," they begged. "We know that we cannot hunt, but while you are busy we will gather sugar-bags from the trees."

"Well," one of the younger Porcupines said to his people, "that might be different. Shall we join them?"

"In view of the fact that you are notoriously unsuccessful in climbing trees, I suggest that you are showing more than your usual sagacity," the oldest Porcupine observed sarcastically.

The men of the two tribes went out together. The Porcupines made a great killing, but by the end of the day the Goannas had not gathered a single sugar-bag. Although they were adept at tree-climbing, they were too lazy to exert themselves in the hot sun. Whenever they saw they were being watched, they pretended to cut foot-holds in the tree trunks, but as soon as the Porcupines' backs were turned, they lay down and went to sleep.

"Never mind," they said at the end of the day. "Honey bags are scarce this year. Now it is time for you to rest. We will cook the food. Go to sleep. We will call you when the food is ready."

The firelight flickered on the leaves of the trees and on the sleeping forms of the Piggiebillahs. Now and then one of them would turn over and ask drowsily, "Is supper ready yet?"

"Not yet. Go to sleep. We will wake you when it is ready."

When the food was cooked, the Mungoongalis scampered up the trees and hid in the foliage. One of them remained behind and threw the roasted bodies of the animals one by one to his companions. While doing so he passed too close to the fire, knocking against a burning log so that it fell on to one of the Piggiebillahs. The Porcupine woke with a scream. The others jumped to their feet and saw the food vanishing into the trees.

One of then snatched a burning stick from the fire and belaboured the Mungoongali. The strokes fell across his golden body, burning the flesh and leaving a pattern of black and yellow stripes which has since been the distinctive coloration of the Goannas.

It is not surprising, therefore, that the Mungoongalis and the Piggiebillahs studiously

avoided each other after that, nor that they entertain the most uncharitable thoughts about each other.

THE GREAT FLOOD

LONG, long ago, before the great flood, the Nurrumbunguttias or spirit men and women lived on earth. They knew that the whole earth was flat, and that for long ages it had been dark, until Pupperrimbul, the Diamond Firetail, a little bird with a red patch on its tail, made the sun. Once that great ball of fire sailed across the sky it gave light and warmth.

Even though the world was warm during the day, the Nurrumbunguttias were cold at night, and they did not like eating raw food, so they made fire to warm themselves and cook their food.

Then came the flood. The water rose up quietly from the sea, until it was higher than the tallest gum tree. It was like a vast blue plain, with only the

55

tops of the mountains standing up above it like islands. The water kept on rising, and finally even the mountain peaks disappeared. The world was one vast, flat sheet of water, and there was no place for the Nurrumbunguttias to live. Many of them were drowned, but others were caught up by a whirlwind which carried them off into the sky, where they became stars, and some, who were gods on earth, became the gods of the sky. Among them was Pund-jil. The Milky Way was made out of the fires that the Nurrumbunguttias had kindled when they were on earth.

Slowly the flood waters receded. The mountain tops appeared again, and the spear heads of trees showed above the water. The sea went back into its own place, and the land steamed under the hot sun.

Animals, birds, insects, and reptiles appeared once more and made their homes on the quickly-drying plains.

Then Kararock and Berwooland Babinger, the son and daughter of Pund-jil, went back to earth and became the first of the true men and women who live in the world today. Wang, who was a star, stole fire from the heavens once more, and gave it to them; and so on earth there were many animals, and men and women to hunt them.

But the spirits of the Nurrumbunguttias, the old spirits of the world, are still alive. It is because of them that we have darkness, storms, and evil spirits in the world today. And remember, if ever a Pupperrimbul, a Diamond Firetail, is killed, another torrent of rain will fall from the skies.

THE HERO WHO WAS CHANGED INTO A MOUNTAIN

ON the Dividing Range the face of a young warrior stares up at the sky. His descendants see the proud profile silhouetted against the setting sun and in their hearts they know that while he remains there, a carved figure in the changeless hills, they will have peace and will be unafraid of their enemies. It is no handiwork of man, this sharp-edged profile. The hand of nature has set it there for all men to see, and to remind the people of the valley that it is to Butcha that they

56

no one had seen him until one morning when he stood on a rock high above the camp and shouted insults and threats.

"Choose the best of your weakling warriors," he called, "and I will cut him into little pieces. Or if you are afraid, come and attack me in force and you will learn the strength of a Baluchi fighting man. Already I have taken many of your wives and young women. Soon no one will be left except old men and women, and babies crying for their mothers' breasts."

Goaded by his words some of the younger men of the tribe hurled themselves up the steep slope, but when they arrived breathless at the rock the Baluchi warrior was no longer there.

The elders sat in conference round the camp fire that night.

"This is a task for young men," they said. "We must accept the challenge or our people will never live in peace. We dare not fail."

They called the young men to them.

"The honour of our tribe is in your hands," they were told. "Who will accept the challenge of the upstart Baluchi people?"

owe their freedom. Cut off in the full strength of manhood, he left no children to remember him and carry on the divine spark of courage and sacrifice to succeeding generations; but there is no need for these while his face can be seen in the dividing hills.

This is the story of how the face of Butcha has been carved into the timeless hills. A fighting man of the Baluchi tribe had made several raids on the Ugarapuls, traversing the pass in the early mornings, killing defenceless men and capturing the most desirable women. The raids were made stealthily and

The young men stepped forward eagerly and a chorus of voices answered, "I will! I will!"

"That is good," an old man grunted. "At least we do not breed cowards among the Ugarapuls. But bravery is not enough. Only one man can be chosen, and we must be sure that he is the most skilful fighter among you. Go to your gunyahs now and sleep with your wives. Sleep well, and in the morning we will choose the one who is to serve us all."

The following morning the eager young warriors danced with excitement. Individual contests were fought, and many a proud young man shed his blood on the grass as he failed to parry the spear of his opponent. There were sore heads and broken legs and arms, but when the sun was high there was no doubt who was most worthy to fight on behalf of the Ugarapuls. It was Butcha who had passed the bora rites so recently that he had not even selected a young woman as his mate.

Before the sun had touched the peaks of the Dividing Range the next day he was on his way. He held the sharp-tipped spears and the polished waddy in his left hand, while a light wooden shield with brightly painted designs rested comfortably on his right arm. He ran nimbly between the trees and was lost to sight in the folds of the hills. When he reached the flat rock where the Baluchi warrior had shouted his challenge the sunlight gilded his body. Standing erect, he heard the distant deep-throated roar of the men of his tribe.

Another sound made him turn his head quickly. It was the fighting man of the Baluchi tribe. He was older than Butcha, his body scarred with ancient wounds, his hair shaggy, the muscles rippling like snakes under his skin. The men stood facing each other like a huge gnarled tree and a young slender sapling growing side by side.

"Come, my little man!" the Baluchi warrior sneered, showing his teeth in a grin and shaking his hair out of his eyes. "Are you the best that the Ugarapul can provide? I expected to find a warrior worthy of my spear this morning."

"Boasting words do not bring victory," Butcha said with a quick smile, dancing lightly from one foot to the other. "The

58

choice fell to me. From this morning's work we will prove whether Ugarapul or Baluchi will dominate this place."

He sprang to one side as the older man lunged at him with his war spear.

The contest will never be forgotten while the camp fires burn at night in the valley of the Ugarapuls. The tribesmen came closer to cheer on their champion, and the men of Baluchi crept out of their hiding places among the trees and rocks.

Time after time Butcha was wounded by spear and club, for the Baluchi warrior was heavier and more experienced in fighting, but his feet still danced as lightly as a bird, and every now and again he penetrated his opponent's guard until the older man was bleeding in a dozen places. The Baluchi man was breathing heavily, and for a moment he lowered his shield. Butcha dropped his spears, seized his waddy in both hands and brought it down on his head with a shattering blow.

For a moment there was silence. It was as though the birds had stopped singing and the wind had died among the trees. A roar of triumph came from the men of Ugarapul. They swarmed over the rock, leaping over the dead body of the fallen warrior, and surrounded their champion. Butcha laughed and threw his arms wide as though to disperse the enemy tribesmen who were stealing away to the shelter of the trees.

With the smile still on his face he swayed and fell, and when they bent over him they found that their young champion was dead. It was only the spirit that had maintained the life in his body until the supreme moment when his club descended on the Baluchi warrior's head and his people were assured of victory.

So he was buried in honour and in sorrow, the young man who sacrificed his life and the children he had yet to father, to save his people. No one knows where his bones are buried. There is no need to know while his face smiles as he lies on his back on the summit of the Dividing Range and shows a proud profile against the blue sky. He remains there in the clear, cold air, a god of the mountain heights whose memory is enshrined in the hearts of his people.

Long before there were men or animals in Australia, the only living things that had eyes to see the vast continent were flocks of migratory birds. When they returned to their homeland they told the animals, who at that time had the form of men and women, of the endless plains, the tree-covered mountains, the wide, long rivers, and the abundant vegetation of the delectable land. Their reports created such excitement that the animals assembled from far and near and held a corroboree. After the singing and dancing was over it was decided that, as the land seemed to be so much more desirable than their own, they would all go to live there.

The problem was how to reach the land of promise. Each animal had its own canoe, but they were frail craft, suited to the placid waters of streams and rivers, but not to the ocean that lay between the two lands. The only vessel that was strong enough, and able to hold them all at once, was the one that belonged to Whale. When he was asked if he would lend it to them, he gave a flat refusal.

The animals decided to take Whale's canoe by force, or by strategem if he would not give it willingly. They enlisted the aid of Starfish, who was Whale's closest friend. Starfish consented, for he was as anxious as the others to make the journey.

"Greetings, my friend," he said to Whale.

"Greetings to you, little Starfish," Whale replied in his deep, rumbling voice. "What do you want?"

"There is nothing I want except to help you, Whale. I see you are badly infested with lice, and I thought that as I am so small I could pick them off for you."

"That's extraordinarily kind of you. They do worry me a bit," Whale admitted.

He placed his head in Starfish's lap and gave a sensuous wriggle of contentment. Starfish picked off the lice in a leisurely manner, taking so long over it that eventually Whale became restless.

"Where is my canoe?" he asked anxiously. "I can't see it."

"It is here, right beside you," Starfish replied soothingly.

He picked up a piece of wood

and struck it against a hollow log by his side, so that it gave a booming sound.

"Are you satisfied now?"

Whale sank back again and submitted himself to his friend's attention.

While the task of cleansing went on, the animals tiptoed to the shore, loaded all their possessions into the huge canoe, and paddled out to sea. The faint splash of their paddles was drowned by Starfish as he scratched busily at the vermin.

"I must not let them get too far away," he thought, "or I will never find them when I swim out to the canoe after dark."

The sun was low when Whale woke up a second time and said, "I am anxious about my canoe. Let me see it."

He brushed Starfish aside and rolled over so that he could look round. There was a long furrow in the sand where the canoe had been pushed into the water, but the canoe was gone. Whale turned round in alarm and saw the canoe almost out of sight in the distance. He turned fiercely on Starfish and attacked him until his old friend was torn to pieces. Starfish resisted as well

as he could, and managed to gouge a furrow in Whale's head, but before long his limbs and torn flesh were tossed contemptuously aside. His descendants hide amongst the rocks as Starfish did, but they still bear in their bodies the marks that Whale inflicted on their ancestor on the day that the animals left their own land for Australia.

Whale raced across the ocean with vapour roaring from the hole in his head. Slowly he began to overtake the canoe. The terrified animals dug their paddles deep in the water and strained every muscle to make the canoe go faster, but it was mainly through the efforts of Kookaburra that they managed to keep a safe distance from the infuriated pursuer.

For several days and nights the chase went on until land came in sight. It was the country they had longed for. At the entrance to Lake Illawarra the canoe grounded and the animals jumped ashore. As they disappeared into the bush the canoe rose and fell on the waves. Brolga, the Native Companion, was the only one who had the presence of mind to realise that they would never be safe while

61

Whale was free to roam the seas in his canoe, for at any time he might come ashore and pursue them again.

Brolga jumped into the canoe and stamped on the thin bark until it broke and sank under the waves. It turned to stone and can now be seen as the island of Ganman-gang off the coast of New South Wales.

Whale turned aside in disgust and swam up the coast, as his descendants have done ever since. As for the animals, they explored the land and found it as good as the birds had said. They settled there, making their homes in trees and caves, by rivers and lakes, in the bush, and in the wide deserts of the interior.

HOW BATS AND SHAGS WERE MADE

BUTHERA, a strong, proud warrior who possessed magical powers, was travelling up the coast of Queensland. He had not gone far on his way, and was resting early in the day, when a man walked into the glade where he was sitting.

"Who are you?" asked Buthera.

"My name is Mudichera. I am the leader of Bats. What are you doing in my land?"

Buthera sprang to his feet, his brows drawn down in a frown.

"This is still my territory. I allow no man to intrude on it."

The stranger took his waddy from his belt.

"Good!" Buthera said. "I am glad to see you are a man and not something blown here by the west wind."

They circled round each other warily. Buthera did not deign to use his waddy or war spear, but held a flint knife in his hand. Mudichera swung his waddy lustily, but Buthera avoided it, jumping from side to side, and throwing himself flat on the ground as it whistled over him. Mudichera began to grow tired. His blows lost their force and he had difficulty in raising his weapon over his head. Buthera gathered himself together and swung his knife so viciously that Mudichera was cut in two pieces, the upper part of his body falling in one place and his legs in another.

There was a flapping of leathery wings, the two parts of his body rose in the air, and two bats escaped from under Buthera's hand. The chief grinned, picked up his weapon and resumed his journey. He covered many miles that day, but the sun grew hotter and the sweat trickled down his back. He felt sick, and when he came to a fertile valley with many water holes, where a large tribe was camped, he stopped.

"Here comes Buthera," the people cried.

"How do you know my name?"

"Oh, we know all about you. We know how you fought with Mudichera, how you cut him in two, and how he changed into a Bat."

"Two Bats. But how do you know all this?"

"Willy Wagtail told us."

Buthera was angry to think that they knew so much about him. He took his magic spear and pointed it in front of him. A long tongue of flame shot from the point and set fire to the scrub. He swung it round him until he was in the centre of the fire, which spread rapidly outwards, driving the screaming people in front of it. The only places where they could escape the flames were in the water holes. Buthera looked across the smouldering bushes and saw them peering appre-

hensively at him, with their bodies submerged in the water. He grinned again, pointed another spear at them, and had the satisfaction of seeing them all transformed into Shags.

Shortly afterwards he met another warrior, but this time he met his match. Larna was young and vigorous, and before long Buthera lay dead at his feet. He picked Buthera up, lifted him above his head, and was on the point of throwing him into a lake, when the Bats who had once been Mudichera flew down and beat their wings round Larna's head, until he was forced to lower the body.

Some of the power that had belonged to Mudichera when he was a warrior lingered in the Bats, and they turned Larna into a stone which they left by the side of the lake as a memorial to Buthera the warrior.

HOW BLACK SNAKE BECAME POISONOUS

MANY years ago the Goannas were much bigger than they are today. They were terrifying creatures, because they were aggressive and possessed poison sacs. The aborigines lived in constant fear of them, and with good cause, because any solitary traveller was liable to be seized by a Goanna, poisoned so that he could not move, and eaten at leisure. When travelling, men and women usually went together in strong bands, fully armed. But sometimes it was necessary for a man to travel from one tribe to another, and from such a hazardous journey he would seldom return.

The animals were unhappy that the human race was in such peril, and they feared for their own lives. If the Goannas were unable to get enough human food, they turned to the lesser animals. They were so big and their hunger so insatiable that it was feared that animals as well as men and women might soon vanish from the earth.

Kangaroo called them all together and asked if anyone could devise a plan to kill the Goannas or render them harmless. Ouyouboolooey, the harmless Black Snake, spoke up at once.

"I will volunteer to do battle with Mungoongali, the chief of the Goannas," he said.

Everyone laughed.

"It will need someone a good deal stronger than you, Ouyouboolooey."

Black Snake was angry.

"You think because I am gentle and harmless I am no use, but I will show you."

He slithered away and eventually arrived at the camp of Mungoongali. It was night time. He came out into the light of the camp fire and said humbly, "Greetings, great Goanna."

"Who are you?" Mungoongali asked, baring his fangs.

"I am only Ouyouboolooey, sir. No one takes any notice of me—and I am not very good to eat," he added hastily.

"Very well. So long as you don't get in my way you can lie

by the fire tonight. Why have you come here?"

"I am trying to find some place where I can live peaceably, without being persecuted by the other animals."

"See that you don't get in my way, then, or it will be the worse for you."

In the morning Mungoongali got up, shook himself, picked up his waddy, and went off into the bush without even glancing at his visitor. Ouyouboolooey was pretending to be asleep. Unobtrusively he slid under the bushes, following closely behind Mungoongali. He saw Goanna crash through the bushes and rush at a solitary traveller who was still sleeping by the ashes of his fire. He crushed his head with a blow of his waddy, hoisted him on his back, and returned to his own encampment.

Ouyouboolooey was there before him, still pretending to be asleep. Mungoongali kicked him out of the way. He placed his poison sac on the ground beside him and dug his sharp teeth into the flesh of the man he had killed.

Like a flash of lightning Ouyouboolooey uncoiled his body, darted forward, seized the poison sac in his mouth,

and vanished into the bushes. He chuckled to himself as he heard Mungoongali thrashing about in the bushes with his waddy, trying to find him.

The council meeting held by Kangaroo was still in session when Black Snake returned.

"Look!" he cried, and distended his jaws so that everyone could see the poison sac.

They crowded round him, congratulating him on his skill and bravery. After a while Kangaroo grew impatient.

"We are proud of you, Ouyouboolooey," he said, "but it is time we went back to our own homes. Now we can live

without fear. Spit out the poison, Black Snake, and we will throw it into the river."

"Oh no," Ouyouboolooey said with a hiss of spite. "You all despised me. You did not think I could get the better of Mungoongali, but it was my skill that did it. Now I have the poison. If anyone dares to come near me, he will die."

The animals recoiled in dismay, and Ouyouboolooey disappeared into the shade of the bushes. He likes solitary places, for he does not have the courage of Goannas, but men and animals fear him because he possesses the deadly poison that was once owned by Goanna.

As for Mungoongali, he dwindled in size after his defeat by Black Snake, and is now an inoffensive reptile which minds its own business and leaves everyone alone.

HOW BLUE HERON BRINGS IN THE TIDE

It was the time to gather the eggs of the geese that were nesting in the swamp. When Muradja, the head man, lit a fire and made smoke signals on the plain, hundreds of men, women, and children came streaming in from the hunting grounds. Every one enjoyed the goose-egg gathering, for they knew they would soon have full bellies and a supply of eggs to trade with more distant tribes. Coolamons and bags would be overflowing when the gathering was over, and every morning and evening the cooking fires on the edge of the swamp would send tall columns of smoke into the still air. The smell of cooking would make their nostrils quiver, and after the feasting was over there would be games and singing and dancing while the elders sat in their solemn councils and looked tolerantly at the pranks of the young people.

And so, as had happened more times than the memory of the oldest man could recall, the geese provided food and prosperity for the tribes, and Muradja was satisfied with the egg-gathering.

The eggs were examined carefully each night while the elders debated whether the chicks were forming. That would be a sign that the egg-laying season was nearing its end, the time when children and young people would be told that they must eat no more. After that the eggs would be reserved for the elders.

"This is the day," Muradja announced at last. "You have fed well, as I can see from your sleek bellies. Soon we will be returning to our own hunting grounds. You may take your surplus supplies with you for trading, but no longer may you eat the goose eggs. You will find a few of them left in the nests. Bring them to the council and go in peace."

That night Windjedda, the son of Muradja, argued with his father. He was a bold youth, spoiled by too much attention from the women. He was not a man, for his initiation into the ranks of the men still lay in the future.

"Why?" he asked his father. "Why should we not eat while the eggs remain?"

"If we ate them all there would be no geese next year, and that would mean no eggs," Muradja replied gently.

"But you eat them—you and the old men."

"It is a privilege that the years have brought to us, my son. Some day you may be head man of the egg-gathering, and it will be your privilege too."

"I don't see why I shouldn't have them now. It won't matter if no one else knows. My belly is not full yet."

"You are a foolish boy," his father reproved him. "When you are ready for your testing you will learn that appetite is the first thing you must control. If you can't do that you will never learn to control pain and fear, and until that time comes you will not be a man."

"I do not fear pain," Windjedda boasted.

"We'll put it to the test now," his father said quietly, "unless you stop talking and let me go to sleep. I said you were a foolish boy, and every word you speak confirms my thought. If you ate any more eggs after the council had forbidden it, they would turn to poison in your belly and you would die."

Windjedda knew that he had gone far enough. He lay down by the fire, but in the flickering firelight he grinned at the thought that his father expected him to believe such nonsense. He knew that it was all an old man's tale, made up so that they could eat as much as they liked. Making plans to outwit them, he fell asleep with the smile still on his face.

The next morning, when the men had left to hunt wallabies, or to fish, he stepped out of the swamp reeds where he had been hiding. Looking round to see that he was not observed, he stole over to the fire where an old woman was cooking eggs for the council.

"Give me one of the eggs," Windjedda demanded.

The old woman looked at him in astonishment.

"You heard what your father said yesterday, Windjedda. There are no more eggs for you, or me, or anyone except the elders."

"Give me that one," he repeated, pointing at the largest egg. "I am hungry. No one will know."

The old woman brandished her stick at him.

"You are an evil boy. I will not let you break our tribal customs."

Windjedda snatched up a fresh egg and broke it over his head. With the contents of the egg running down his face, he hurried to the beach where Muradja was spearing fish and cried, "Look what the old woman has done to me! Do you allow this to happen to your son?"

The head man was angry at the insult offered to his son. If he had paused to consider the matter he would have realised that Windjedda was not to be trusted. In that case he would have called a council meeting, and the truth would have been discovered. Anger distorts a man's judgment, and so it was with Muradja.

Muttering spells, he ran up the beach, jabbing the air with his spear, followed closely by the delighted Windjedda. At his feet the tide gurgled and raced over the sand. It did not stop at the high tide mark. It sped over the dry land, lapped at the sandhills, turning them into islands, and raced through the scrub towards the big encampment. The fires steamed momentarily until they were quenched by the flood waters.

The women and children ran to a big banyan tree and climbed up it, but the water rose until the tree was covered, and they were washed away and drowned. The fishermen and hunters met the same fate. Only Muradja and Windjedda escaped. They were transformed into Blue Herons, the birds which run before the advancing tide on the shores of the Timor Sea to this very day.

68

"I SHALL die of thirst," Koala said to his friend Kangaroo.

"I know," replied Kangaroo. "I am bigger than you, and I need more water. What shall we do?"

"There's nothing we can do except sit in the shade of the trees and wait till death comes. The sky has forgotten to rain, and there is no water left."

"That is not a proper way to meet death," Kangaroo reproved him. "We are warriors. We should be ashamed to sit down and weep like women. Anyway, there is not enough water left in my body to cry with," he added. "Listen, Koala. Far away, by the distant hills, there used to be a river. If we went there we might find a water hole in the bed of the river."

"Come on then," Koala replied wearily, but his spirits rose a little at his friend's words of hope.

They plodded across the plain together. The sun beat down on them, making their fur stiff and uncomfortable. Behind them two sets of footprints stretched farther and farther into infinity. Sometimes they passed pathetic little bundles of fur and bones, which were all that was left of the bodies of other animals and birds. Their tongues were dry and swollen, and when they panted for breath the hot air seared their lungs.

At night they lay exhausted on the hot sand, and woke in the morning feeling cold and stiff until the sun rose to warm them again. Early in the afternoon they dragged themselves to the bank of the river. Their fur was full of dust and brittle stalks of dried grass. Wherever they looked the earth was bare and baked dry, while the river bed was as uninviting as the plain they had crossed.

"Where are the water holes you talked about?" Koala asked bitterly.

"I didn't say there were any water holes. If you had listened you would know that I said that there might be some water here. Obviously there is none. But cheer up. I remember something my mother told me many years ago that saved her life in time of drought. Sometimes, if only you can find the right place, you can dig a deep hole and water will seep down and fill it. Let's try."

"You begin," Koala said. "I'm too tired, but I'll help you later." He curled up and went to sleep, while Kangaroo searched until he found a place where there might be some water, and began to dig with his strong claws. He threw earth and sand up in a big circle and gradually sank from sight into the hole he was digging.

After a long time he climbed out and shook Koala till he woke.

"It is your turn now," he said. "I am exhausted."

"Did you find any water, Kangaroo?"

"Not yet. In fact the soil isn't even damp, but I'm sure we'll get some if we keep on digging."

"I'm not ready yet, Kangaroo. Please leave me alone. The sun has burnt all the life out of me. I feel sick. I think I'm going to die."

Kangaroo looked down at his friend. Koala looked so small and miserable that he felt sorry for him. Without another word he went back to the hole, and soon handfuls of dirt flew out as he resumed his digging.

His heart gave a jump as he felt damp earth under his paws. He dug faster, and then went and sat on the pile of earth that he had excavated. The afternoon light was beginning to fade, but he could see a faint gleam at the bottom of the hole. The evening breeze sprang up and the water shivered.

Koala was pretending to be asleep. Kangaroo bent over him and whispered, "I have found water! Wait here and I will bring you some."

Koala sprang to his feet, knocked against Kangaroo and sent him sprawling on the ground as he rushed to the hole and disappeared from sight.

Kangaroo limped across the river bed and peered down at the water hole. Koala was at the bottom greedily lapping water without a thought for his companion who had done all the work. At last he realised how selfish his little friend had been. Koala had left him to do all the hard work, and when success had come, he had thought only of himself. A surge of anger made his fur stand on end.

He took his stone knife and climbed silently down into the hole. Koala's tail stretched out behind, quivering in ecstasy as the cool water ran down his throat. The sight goaded Kangaroo into action. Raising the knife, he brought it down with all his strength, severing it almost at the root.

Koala jumped high in the air with a blood-curdling screech, turned round, and saw his friend brandishing the knife in one hand and holding the tail in the other. He scrambled to his feet, scurried out of the hole, and was lost to sight in the gathering darkness.

Kangaroo buried his head in the water and drank life-giving draughts of cold, sparkling water. Then he threw back his head and laughed and laughed at the thought of Koala running about without a tail.

But Koala doesn't think it funny to go through life without a tail!

HOW PLATYPUS WAS BORN

THE Ducks who lived in a secluded river pond seldom left their home for fear of Mulloka, the Water Devil. Among the Ducks was a young female who was contemptuous of the warnings of her elders.

While everyone was busy one morning she floated quietly out into the stream and drifted along until she reached a patch of green grass. She came close to the bank, waddled up the steep slope, and sat down, enjoying her freedom. Unfortunately she had chosen for her resting place the roof of the home of Water Rat.

Hearing noises above his burrow he came out to investigate, and discovered the young Duck. Water Rat was overjoyed, because for a long time he had been lonely in his riverside home. He crept up behind her and whispered, "Welcome to my home, my lovely darling. I have waited for you for a long time."

Duck shrieked, flapped her wings, and struggled towards the river. Water Rat was annoyed. He prodded her with his spear, and dragged her into his burrow. She huddled against the farthest side of the damp, gloomy hole. Her beak opened and shut, but no sound came out.

Water Rat smiled ingratiatingly.

"You are my prisoner," he said, "but don't be afraid. I will be good to you. See how handsome I am! And my heart is even kinder than my face.

Live here with me and be my wife."

Helpless as she was, Duck had no choice but to accept. Her only hope was that she would be able to make her escape when her repulsive husband was asleep, but soon she became aware that there was little chance of returning to her family and friends. Water Rat had made the position very clear.

"I never sleep during the day," he had told her. "If you are imagining that you can escape by night, remember Mulloka, the Water Devil! Is it not better to remain with me, my pretty little wife, than to be devoured by Mulloka?"

For several weeks Duck stayed in the burrow, but eventually Water Rat grew careless and allowed her to paddle in the water outside.

One sunny day Duck spent a while feeding on water-weed and insects, and returned to the burrow. As soon as she put her head inside she saw that Water Rat had succumbed to the heat, and was lying curled up and snoring.

She paddled outside and fled up the river. On arrival at her home she was greeted excitedly by her family, and

in a few days she had almost forgotten her ordeal.

Presently the time for nest-making and the laying of eggs arrived. The young females hid themselves among the reeds, and before long they floated out, proudly leading the baby ducklings. With them came the young Duck who had been married to Water Rat.

Behind her swam two children ... two little Ducks with duck bills and webbed feet, but alas, they had no feathers. Their bodies were covered with the fur of a Water Rat, and they had four webbed feet instead of two. On their hind legs were sharp spikes which looked like the spear of Water Rat.

The poor mother was taunted by her friends, and in shame and despair she left the sheltered billabong and made a new home for her babies far away from her friends. Her children grew up and became the first of the Gay-dari, the tribe of the Platypus.

HOW THE MURRAY RIVER WAS MADE

Long before the Murray River became a broad torrent of refreshing, life-giving water, an earthquake shook the barren land and formed a long trench or chasm. Occasional rain storms swept across the land, and a tiny stream flowed down the newly-formed rent.

Then came another tremor which caused the hills to shake and the land to dance as though a corroboree was being held far under the earth. Rocks and soil heaved, and from the very bowels of the earth an enormous fish shouldered its way to the surface.

It was borne on the crest of a wave of water. The sun sparkled on the silver torrent which boiled and eddied in the trench, following the trail of the fish which swam down the stream. It was far too large for the narrow bed. It dug its head into the earth and scooped it up on either side, widening its path with strokes of its powerful tail. The water filled the hollows made by the head and tail of the fish, and behind it the broad stream flowed gently with many turns and bends as the agitated water subsided.

So the bulldozer of ancient days excavated the bed of the Murray River and filled it with water as far as Lake Alexandrina.

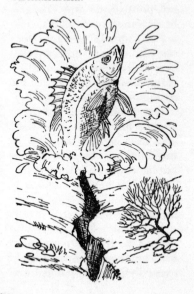

There it was arrested by the hand of Nepelle, the Great Ruler of the heavens. He picked the fish up and cut it into small pieces which he threw back into the river, where they remain as the ponde (Murray cod), pomeri (mud-fish), tarki (perch), tukkeri (a flat, silvery fish), kundegulde (butter-fish), tinuwarre (bream), and mallowe (Murray Mouth salmon).

HOW THE PORCUPINE GOT HIS SPINES

PIGGIEBILLAH the Porcupine was once a man. When he grew old, so old that all his friends had died, he lived with men who had been boys when he was middle-aged. They were all strong and tireless, and able to hunt all through the hot sunny hours of the day, and to travel long distances in search of food, but Piggie-billah was too old to take his part in providing food for the tribe. No one gave him any-thing to eat, and it was sur-prising that he remained so well. As he grew older he seemed better nourished than anyone else. In fact it was so very surprising that some of the people became suspicious and kept a close watch on him. After some time they discovered something that Piggiebillah had kept a secret to himself for years.

When he left the camp one morning, he was followed, and it was seen that he went to a rock at some distance from the encampment, and hid in its shadow. The watchers peered at him from behind bushes, wondering what he was waiting for. They soon found out.

A young woman came along the path. Piggiebillah sprang out, and before anyone could move or give a shout of warn-ing, he plunged his spear into her body. The old man dragged her off the track, ate her limbs, and hid the rest of her body away for a later meal.

The disappearance of many people of their tribe, and of visitors who were expected and never arrived, was at last explained. A secret meeting was held and it was unani-mously decided that Piggie-billah must be killed. He was so active, in spite of his great age, that he had to be taken unawares.

They waited until there was a dark night without a moon. The old man was lying at some distance away from the fire. The men gathered silently round him. He was sleeping on his back with his mouth shut to prevent his spirit from wandering. He moved in his sleep and murmured, "I hear the butterflies stamping in the grass."

While he dreamed of butterflies the men drove their spears into his body. Piggiebillah groaned as they beat him with their clubs. Bone after bone in his body and arms and legs was broken, and at last the terrible cannibal lay still.

His wife was looking on in horror. She hit her head with her digging stick until the blood ran over her breast. Her name was Guineeboo, and when she fled from the scene she became Guineeboo, the Red-breasted Robin.

The men crowded round the fire, laughing and chattering over their easy victory. But Piggiebillah was not dead. He dragged himself painfully into the deeper shadows until he came to the burrow of Trap-door Spider, Murga Muggai. He fell down the hole, and stayed at the bottom until his wounds were healed. The one thing he could not do was to pull the spears out of his body, nor did the bones in his broken limbs knit together.

Nobody recognised Piggiebillah when he came out into the daylight again. He crawled on all fours, with his broken legs splayed out, and the spears were a bristling forest on his back. For food he dug with his hands, and had to be satisfied with ants and other insects, and scraps of food. Piggiebillah had turned into a Porcupine, the little animal that scratches for ants because he cannot eat other food, and burrows underground to escape from his enemies.

HOW POSSUM AND CAT KILLED KANGAROO

KUPERREE was the biggest Kangaroo who ever lived. He was so strong and fierce that he killed many men, and even the great Bunyip was afraid of him. When he bounded across the plain he was so terrible to look at that hunters dropped their weapons and fled into the bush.

Everyone was afraid of him —everyone except Pilla and Inta, who were two brave hunters.

"Let us kill him and put an end to the fear that men have,"

Pilla said, and Inta agreed.

Arming themselves with their best weapons, the hunters went out and found Kuperree's tracks. They followed them as far as a mountain, and when they advanced cautiously through the bush they found the giant animal lying fast asleep under a tree.

Each hunter chose a spear, but when they tested the blades with their thumbs they found that the spear heads were blunt.

"It is your fault," Inta said. "You should have seen that the spears were sharp before we left the camp."

"And what about your own spear?" Pilla asked. "It is no better than mine. You are a fine one to talk!"

The hunters quarrelled so violently that Pilla's nose was flattened against his face. He sprang up and jabbed his spear into Inta again and again until he was bleeding from many wounds.

"Stop! Stop!" Inta shouted. "Look! While we have been fighting Kuperree has woken up!"

It was true. The giant Kangaroo was bounding towards them, and they knew that with one blow of his tail

he could break their backs. They turned to face him, and in spite of their blunt spears, managed to wound him so badly that he fell over and died.

This gave the hunters time to sharpen their knives, and they cut Kuperree open. Inside they found the bodies of many of their friends, some of whom had been mighty hunters. Both Pilla and Inta were wirrinuns. They chanted magic spells which healed the gaping wounds of the other hunters, and brought them back to life. When the men were able to talk they danced round the

76

dead body of Kuperree, lit a big fire, and roasted his flesh, greased themselves all over with his fat, and had a meal at which every part of the giant Kangaroo was eaten up.

After the fight was over, and every one had praised the two brave hunters, they were changed from men into animals, so that everyone would know that they were the killers of Kuperree. Pilla became a Possum, with the furrow down his nose which was made when Inta struck him. Inta became a native Cat, and the white spots on his body are the marks that were made by Pilla's blunt spear.

HOW TORTOISE GOT A SWOLLEN BACK

SWAMP Turtle was in a vicious mood.

"Go and get some gum for my spears," he snapped.

Tortoise tossed her head.

"Go and get it yourself," she retorted. "Why should I fetch and carry for you all the time? I have quite enough work to do here."

Swamp Turtle was speechless with rage. He picked up his waddy and beat her on the back. Some of his blows were so wild that they struck her on the head and legs. She drew in her head and crouched down, until all that was exposed was the broad sweep of her back. Turtle kept hitting her until the poor woman's back was bruised and swollen, and then went off to get the gum himself.

As soon as he had gone Tortoise dragged herself painfully down to the swamp and submerged herself in the cool water. Ever since then her back has remained humped and swollen, and she hides her head under the shell she has grown to protect herself from Swamp Turtle.

HOW TORTOISE LOST HIS TAIL

ACROSS the river of death lay the gigantic tortoise that bridged the gulf between the land of men and the land of souls. The spirits of men were required to cross the river before they could reach the world of eternal life, and the only path by which they could travel lay across the tail of the tortoise. It stretched over the swifty flowing river from one bank to the other.

No one knew what would

happen when death came, and the spirit set out on its long journey to the land of spirits, until a man returned to tell them of his experiences.

"I travelled across a wide plain," he said. "In the distance I saw the gleam of running water and knew that I would have to cross the river. When I came close to it, I saw that the banks were steep, and that no man could hope to live in the rushing torrent. But the way was made plain. There is a giant tortoise by which the souls of men may cross. On the far shore the shell of the tortoise rises up like a moun-

tain, and its head is as big as a small hill. Its mouth is full of sharp white teeth, and its eyes gleam like fire.

"There is no other way to cross. I stepped on to the tail and ran across as quickly as I could, but I had not gone half the distance when the tortoise wriggled and I fell into the river. I was tossed about like a twig and carried into a dark tunnel. I thought I would have died a second time, because I was dashed against rocks, and bruised and cut by their sharp edges. Look, you can see the scars which will tell you better than any words of mine that what I say is true.

"Presently I was carried into the daylight again, and I saw many people playing by the banks of the river, hunting, and gathering firewood. Some of them were our own people who have died, but I do not think that the river is the true land of spirits. It may be that they are still resting before they continue their journey.

"The river swept me past them and carried me into the ocean, where I was battered by the waves, and the salt water stung my wounds. I was washed to and fro. The salt water healed my bleeding body, and after a long time I was thrown up on a sandy beach. When my strength returned I kept the sun on my left side, crossing wide plains and high mountains, until at last I reached my home. You can see for yourselves that I have returned."

"What shall we do?" he was asked. "When the time comes for us to die, how shall we escape the tortoise with the long tail and the wicked head?"

"Someone who is strong and fearless and has the power of the great spirits must take an axe and cut off the tail of the tortoise. Men will then be able to travel the road in safety."

"Who shall it be?" they asked, and they looked at the wirrinun, the sorcerer who lived with them.

"I know you are looking at me," he said with a smile, "and you are relieved that it is me who has the power and not you. Very well. I shall die this night, and I will do as you wish. But when you bury my body you must also bury my axe with me."

The next day the spirit of the wirrinun rose from his body in the newly-dug grave, took his axe, and set out for the river. He went by a circuitous route, and climbed a tall tree, where he sat on a branch, waiting to see what would happen. Far below him the souls of men reached the river bank, looked round them, and when they realised that there was no other way across the river, began to walk along the outstretched tail. Before they reached the opposite bank, the tortoise twitched his tail, and they were shaken off and swept away in the river.

The wirrinun descended the tree, went over to the tip of the tortoise's tail, and ran lightly across it. He sped over like a gust of wind, feeling the sharp jerk as the tortoise tried to shake him off, but he was running so fast that he reached the body of the creature before the tail could swing into action. Turning round, the medicine man gave a terrific blow with his axe and severed the tail at the root. The tortoise reared up, twisted in the air, and fell on the bold wirrinun. But the sorcerer was ready for him. He wriggled clear, the axe descended a second time, and the ghastly head rolled on the ground.

With a sigh of relief, the wirrinun went to a tall tree

and cut it down so that it fell across the river, providing a safe bridge for all the souls who would come that way. At the root of the tree there was a snake which uncoiled its body and flicked its tongue at him. With a final blow he cut off its head.

The body of the tortoise was still quivering, and the wirrinun felt a momentary pang of pity. After all, the creature had but obeyed the will of the great spirits who had designed the pattern of the universe, and had appointed him as the pathway for men's souls. It was destiny that had brought him to this place and had changed the passage of souls for all the days to come. The tortoise had been the unwitting instrument of fate, and the hulk that lay helpless on the river bank had not acted of its own volition.

The wirrinun could not restore its tail, but the snake's head still lay by the tree stump. He picked it up, cut off the poison fangs with his knife, and joined it to the stump of the tortoise's neck.

That is why every tortoise has a short, stumpy tail and the head of a snake.

HOW TORTOISE GOT HIS SHELL

THEY had chosen a wife for Wayamba, but he was disgruntled. There was nothing attractive about her, and Wayamba had his own ideas of the kind of wife he wanted. He refused to look at her, let alone take her into his wurley. Instead he went off to the neighbouring tribe, the Oolah or Spiny Lizards. Hiding himself in the bushes, he kept watch for most of the day observing the young women. One in particular fascinated him. She carried herself erect and had a bold, twinkling eye. And she was a good worker. Wayamba's heart seemed to play tricks in his body when she left her friends and came towards him. It was almost as though she knew he was there.

No one else was looking. Wayamba jumped out of the bushes, put his hand over her mouth, and half led, half carried her into the scrub. He forced her on to the ground and crouched down, listening for sounds of pursuit, but the only sounds that came to his ears were those of normal tribal life. Apparently no one had noticed the abduction of the young woman.

He looked at her closely. Her body was firm and lean, her legs and arms shapely, and her face was bearable. Some say that she was a married woman with three children, but whether it be true or not, she was an attractive young woman.

"If you scream I will stun you with my waddy," he warned her, and cautiously took his hand away from her mouth.

The girl smiled and touched his arm.

"Why should I scream?" she asked. "I have seen many men, but none I like better than you."

Wayamba grinned and caught her to him.

"You will be my wife," he said hoarsely.

After several days Wayamba and his Oolah wife went home to his tribe.

"Who is that you have with you?" he was asked.

"This is Oolah, a wife I have chosen for myself."

"But what about the wife we gave you? You cannot flout the tribal laws and choose your own wife, Wayamba."

"You can take her away. Do what you like with her. I have never touched her. Someone else can marry her for all I care. This is my true wife."

"How did you get the woman? Was she given to you?"

The young woman looked up at her husband coyly. He threw out his chest and said defiantly, "I stole her from the Spiny Lizard tribe."

A low wail came from the women who had gathered round to hear what was said.

"They will punish you. Grief will come to our tribe."

"Don't worry," Wayamba said. "They will leave you alone. I can take care of myself."

He grinned at them and took his young wife into his wurley.

The next morning the warriors of the Oolah arrived.

"Where is our daughter?" they shouted.

The men and women of Wayamba's tribe remained seated round their fire, muttering to themselves, and took no notice of the threatening gestures of the newcomers.

There was a loud shout and they all turned towards the wurley where Wayamba was standing. He had tied a shield to the front of his body and another on his back, and was brandishing his weapons.

"Your child is here in my wurley. She is my true wife now, and I will not allow you to take her back. I took her by force, and by force I will keep her."

The Oolahs rushed forward and hurled their spears at Wayamba. They rattled against his shield and glanced harmlessly aside. Some of the spear throwers crept behind him, only to find that his back was as well protected as his chest and stomach.

Wayamba threw back his head and roared with laughter.

"Come and do your worst! You have met your match for once, Oolahs!"

His words infuriated the warriors. Their spears were all gone, but they surged against the young man, raining blows on his head and limbs. He found himself being overwhelmed. He dodged to and fro trying to avoid the blows. Seeing an opening, he rushed through it, leaving his wife behind, and dived into the river.

He was never seen again, but after the Oolahs had taken the young woman away, a funny creature climbed out of the river. It had an oval shell which covered its body, but its head and limbs projected beyond it. It waddled along the bank and disappeared in the distance, moving on the ground like a flat stone. It was Wayamba the Tortoise, who always carries his armour with him to protect him from his enemies.

HOW THE WARATAH WAS MADE

BAHMAI crept stealthily along the war trail, his eyes fixed on the back of the warrior in front of him, ready to throw himself into the scrub and lie so still that not even the birds could see him. He grasped his war spear and waddy a little more firmly than was necessary, for he had only just passed the initiation tests, and this was his first raiding expedition. The scars were still fresh, but he had forgotten the pain that racked his body in the excitement of the moment. He was not conscious of his lean figure and the rippling muscles that had won him admiring glances from the young women of his tribe. His training, the ordeals that he had passed through, all the experiences of his young life were gathered together and concentrated in mind and muscle on this wonderful day when at last he was to meet the ultimate test of manhood. He shook his head to clear the red mist that floated before his eyes—a red mist of hatred and exultation that flooded his mind as he thought of the vengeance that would be exacted on the nomadic tribe that had invaded the tribal territory.

If he had looked behind and up the slopes of the hill he would have seen a bright patch of colour among the rocks. The leader of the war party had looked at it with narrowed eyes, and then had turned away, recognising it as the wallaby skin garment adorned with red feathers that belonged to Krubi, one of the younger women of the tribe. For a moment he had wondered why she was there, and then dismissed the thought. It was his responsibility to see and interpret every unusual sight or movement; but Bahmai was young and inexperienced, and had no eyes or ears for anything but the trail and the longed-for moment of battle.

With an intensity that matched his own, Krubi stared down at Bahmai until he was lost to sight among the trees farther down the valley. She had loved him even before his initiation, and now that he had become a man, her body seemed on fire with longing and tenderness.

As the last warrior disappeared from sight, she settled herself in a comfortable position to wait for the return of the raiders. The hot sun seemed to set the rocks on fire, lizards lay motionless, the leaves of the trees hung limply in the still air. The whole world was asleep, but Krubi remained awake, straining her eyes for the first sign of the returning warriors. When the fighting was over, and his spear was reddened with blood, she knew that Bahmai would look up and see her, and that she would be glad because she had waited for him. She knew that the sight of her cloak and feathers would send the blood dancing in his veins, and that soon he would claim her as his wife, and no one would forbid him.

The shadows were lengthening as a tiny procession of dark figures emerged from the bush.

There were fewer men than in the morning, and they walked slowly with none of the quivering energy of a few hours before. They were too far away for Krubi to see their faces, but she would recognise her lover by his slim body, the way he walked, and by the lifting of his head as he sought her among the rocks and bushes of the hillside.

One by one the men came into full view, but Bahmai was not among them. Her hands dropped to her side and at that moment she faced the reality that comes to women who cannot relieve their feelings in action, but must wait and sorrow in anguish. She sank to the ground and buried her face in her hands, heedless of the little world of insects and reptiles and birds that were bold enough to approach her.

In the morning her people came to take her back to the camp, but she would not move, and refused food when it was offered to her. Each day they returned, but Krubi was as unresponsive to their pleading as one of the boulders on the hillside. Her tears trickled between her fingers and dropped on the stony ground, forming a tiny rivulet which flowed down into the valley. The moistened earth sprang to life, and grass and flowers bloomed along the course of the stream.

On the seventh day she stood up, slim and straight as Bahmai her lover had been, and sank slowly into the ground. She disappeared from sight, but the tiny creek still flowed, chattering and singing a song of love and longing.

Krubi, for love of her own dead warrior, had left the world as he had done. Long days and nights followed. Underground there was a stirring of new life, roots drew nourishment from the stream, a tender shoot pushed its way between the stones and grew into a tree which became as strong and slender as Bahmai had ever been. It put forth leaves that were like the reddened points of Bahmai's spear, and then a flower that glowed on the hillside like a second sun. It was redder than Krubi's wallaby skin garment —as red as the cockatoo feathers that had adorned it.

The tree was the waratah whose leaves remind us of Bahmai's spear, whose flaming red flowers are the symbol of the love of Krubi and Bahmai.

84

As the waratah flower became the symbol of undying love, so the name Krubi was reserved for girls who possessed beauty of face and character. Only one woman of the tribe was allowed to bear the coveted name. It was not until one Krubi died that it could be conferred on a new baby. When that time came there was great competition amongst young mothers to win the privilege of naming their own girl baby after the lubra who had become the first waratah.

Because there was so much jealousy on these occasions, it happened that the spirit of love and devotion that surrounded the name was sometimes lost to sight.

The Krubi of the time of our story was a very old woman, and her powers were failing. When the tribe moved to a new camp in search of game, she found it increasingly difficult to carry the bag that contained her few personal possessions. Krubi was frightened. In spite of her great age she enjoyed the busy life of the camp, and she feared that when her husband saw her frailty, he would put her

away and leave her in the care of their youngest daughter Woolyan. When that time came she knew that she would be subjected to many indignities, and would lose the respect of her friends. When the camp was shifted she clutched her dilly bag with trembling fingers, and willed her feet to carry her emaciated body, but the effort was too much for her, and she sank down with a groan.

Woolyan had been following her mother. A cruel smile curved her lips when she saw that the old woman was helpless. She made no attempt to assist her, but stood looking down at her mother.

"Help me up," Krubi begged. "My husband must not see me like this."

"You will have to help yourself," Woolyan replied. "My baby will soon be born. It is enough for me to carry her in my body without dragging you along too."

The old woman looked up at her daughter with a pleading expression, but Woolyan hardened her heart. She hoped that her baby would be a girl, and that she would be allowed to

85

call her Krubi, but she knew that while her mother lived she would not be allowed to do so, and that if the child was given another name, the opportunity would be lost for ever.

Krubi read her thoughts. A gust of anger shook her body. She scrambled to her feet, seized her bag, and with a fresh access of strength plodded resolutely along the path and eventually caught up with her husband.

Woolyan bit her lip until the blood trickled down her chin. Her heart was filled with unreasoning anger. That night she looked closely at her mother in the light of the camp fire and realised that the fright that Krubi had received had given her new life.

An evil thought came into her mind. She remembered the occasions when the men had pointed the bone at an enemy and had sent the spirit away from his body.

"If only I could do that to old Krubi!" she thought. She did not realise that this power was given only to men who had earned the right to use it through years of training, and by subjecting themselves to prolonged ordeals. She knew that the privilege was forbidden to women, but the desire to confer the wonderful name on her unborn child was so great that she became reckless.

She found a bone, polished it until it was smooth, and went to seek her mother. It was dark, but she could see the old woman lying asleep in her miamia. Taking the bone from where she had hidden it, she pointed it at the defenceless woman and began to mutter spells she had been taught when she was initiated to womanhood; but they were powerless, and the bone dropped from her fingers. Krubi woke up, and in a moment of enlightenment realised what her daughter was doing. Fear gave her strength. She bounded to her feet, snatching the bone from Woolyan as the young woman bent to pick it up. Clutching it desperately in her gnarled hands, she used it to beat her daughter over the head, until Woolyan cried for mercy.

Her cries roused the camp. The men rushed to Krubi's miamia, separated the two women, and listened to what the old lady had to say. There was a shocked silence when they realised that Woolyan had tried to kill her mother with a pointing bone.

Late into the night the elders debated the terrible deed that Woolyan had done, and passed sentence on her.

"You are to go into the bush," they said. "Wait for us there until we come to you."

Woolyan knew that she was to be killed. Slowly she left the camp and went into a glade where the waratah trees were in full bloom. They seemed to smile at her in the darkness, and the scent was heavy on the night air. Like water it washed away her evil thoughts. She knelt at the foot of the trees and sobbed with relief as the flowers of love drove the bitter-

ness and jealousy from her heart. And as she knelt there, her baby was born.

When the men came to put her to death, a strange radiance filled the grove, and they felt the atmosphere of serenity. The baby was gurgling contentedly. Woolyan stood up and faced them.

"I am ready," she said quietly. "I have done wrong, and you have come to punish me. Please look after my baby. When she grows to womanhood, bring her to this place and tell her that her mother repented of the wicked things she had done."

The leader of the men said abruptly, "Bring Krubi here."

The old lady was brought into the grove. She saw her daughter standing in front of the trees, and her granddaughter lying on the grass. Impetuously she ran forward and put her arms round Woolyan. Their tears mingled and dropped one by one on the red flowers.

The chief threw away his club and went up to them. The scent of the waratah blooms attracted his attention. He lifted one of the flowers and put it to his lips. A delighted smile spread over his face. The tears of repentance and forgiveness had flavoured the flower, which tasted of honey.

Perhaps the baby girl was called Krubi when her grandmother died. We do not know; but we do know that since that dark night when passions were released and dispersed by the scent of the flowers, the waratah blooms have been as sweet as the honey of bees.

HOW TREE-RUNNER MADE A RAINBOW FOR HIS WIFE

BIBBY had fallen in love with little Deereeree, although she was a widow and had four children. He courted her, telling her how much he loved her, but every time he asked her to marry him and come to live in his camp, she looked sorrowful, and said, "No, Bibby. I cannot leave my children."

"Bring them with you," Bibby would say, puffing out his chest. "I am strong enough to look after you and your children, and to give you all the food you need."

But Deereeree could not be persuaded. She was afraid of Bibby. She was afraid of the trees that rustled and swayed over her when the wind blew, afraid of the big animals that came to the water hole when she went to get water for her children, afraid of storms, and wind, and rain. Afraid most of all of the dark nights, and the spirits that waited in the shadows beyond the firelight.

All night long Bibby could hear her crying her own name, "Wyah, wyah, Deereeree, Deereeree."

He longed to go to her, gather her up in his arms, and comfort her, but he knew that if he appeared out of the darkness she would die of fright.

Every morning he visited her

and brought food for her and her babies. She was grateful, and sometimes she longed to take shelter by Bibby's camp fire, to know that she had a strong husband to protect her. Often she was on the point of saying "Yes" when he pressed her to marry him, but then she was overcome by fear once more. He was so big and strong that she was frightened of what he might do to her and the children.

At last Bibby could no longer stand the thin, mournful cry that came from Deereeree's camp. He was a builder. He made the biggest, stoutest building of his whole life. Beginning far away at the foot of the mountains, it reached up to the sky in a smooth arch, and then down again in the same smooth curve which ended not far from Deereeree's camp. He painted it with the most beautiful colours the world has ever seen, and then, when the labour was over, he called to the woman he loved.

"Deereeree, come and see what I have made! It is a road that leads from the earth up to the sky and down again, and it is all for you."

Deereeree peered cautiously out of her wurley, with the children poking their heads out under her arms.

"What is it?" she asked in a tiny voice.

"It is Yulu-wiree the Rainbow," Bibby said proudly.

"Oh Bibby, will it hurt me?"

"If you will be my wife it will not hurt you," Bibby replied. "It will be a road that we can walk together. But," he added sternly, "if you refuse to marry me it may fall down and crush you. You, and all your children."

Deereeree ran to him.

"You are so strong, so wise, Bibby," she said, holding tightly to him. "I know you love me. Take me to your home where I will be safe."

Bibby proudly bore her away, and the children scuttled after them. He was a good husband and a proud father to Deereeree's children. They lived happily together until the children grew up and left them, and married girls of their own age.

But when Bibby died and Deereeree was left alone, her fears returned. At night the old quavering cry came from the camp—"Wyah, wyah, Deereeree, Deereeree."

They lived long ago, these two, but Bibby will always be remembered, because he is

Bibby the Tree-runner who made the Rainbow. And of course Deereeree will never be forgotten, because she is the little Willy Wagtail whose mournful night cry, "Wyah, Deereeree" can still be heard.

KANGAROO AND EMU

BOHRA the Kangaroo had taken Dinewan the Emu to wife, but Dinewan was discontented. The ways of the Kangaroo tribe were different to those of her own tribe, and she was often restless.

One night, while Bohra was asleep, she picked fretfully at the grass and leaves in the roof of the wurley. Her husband was woken up by twigs falling on his face.

"What are you doing?" he asked.

"Nothing."

He went to sleep again, but was wakened once more, and lay still to find out the cause of the rain of twigs and leaves that was falling on him. In the gloom he could see Dinewan pulling out the twigs and throwing them on the ground. Other leaves and small fragments of bark and wood fell out. It was these that had woken him as they pattered down on his face and body.

"Dinewan!" he said sharply. "Why are you doing that?"

She sighed, and said in-differently, "Why shouldn't I? There's nothing else to do."

"Don't be ridiculous. This is the time for sleeping."

"But the night is so long. I'm tired of the darkness."

"I can't help that. It has nothing to do with me."

"Oh Bohra," she said, snuggling up to him, "you are so clever, you can do anything. Before we were married you told me that you were a famous wirrinun."

"I am," Bohra said. "There is no more powerful medicine man in all these parts."

"I knew you were clever! Take me to a place where there is no darkness."

Grumbling a little, Bohra led his wife outside, and they stumbled through the scrub, looking for light in the darkness. Before long Dinewan began to wish that she had never left the wurley. She bumped against trees, bruised her shins on rocks and stumps, and trod on thorns and prickles until she could bear the pain no longer. She rubbed one foot against the other, but it only made matters worse. The skin came off the lower part of her legs, and big lumps rose on her feet. That is why Emus have such bare, ugly legs.

"I can't go any farther," she said, dropping to the ground. "If you are such a wonderful wirrinun we wouldn't be looking for light in this horrible bush. You'd drive the darkness away."

Bohra grunted.

"If you really loved me, that's what you would do!" she pleaded.

"Try to go to sleep. I'll see what I can do."

They drifted off to sleep. Bohra's spirit left his body and travelled far to the east. There it lifted up the curtain of the dark and began to roll it across the sky. The light grew stronger. At first trees were silhouetted against the light sky, then gleams of sunlight caught the distant hills, colour came into the foliage, and birds began to sing.

Even in her sleep Dinewan was anxious to miss nothing. She kept one eye and one ear open all the time. When she grew tired she closed them and opened the other eye and ear —and that is how Emus have slept from that night onwards.

The wandering spirit returned to Bohra's body. He opened his eyes and looked at the sunlit landscape.

"There you are, my dear," he said to Dinewan. "My spirit has done this, so I have done it too. The spirit and I are the same being. From now on we who are Kangaroos will be able to see in the dark as well as in the light, but as for you, all I can do is to make the night shorter."

Dinewan smiled to herself, knowing that she would be able to keep an eye and an ear on Bohrah, even in the darkest night.

THE KANGAROO DANCE

BOHRAH was the name of Kangaroo when he was only a four-footed animal creeping through the grass on the plains of New South Wales. One night he saw the flickering flames of camp fires in the distance, and heard the shouts of two-legged men. He was curious to know what was happening. Creeping stealthily through the darkness, he came close to the encampment and watched the scene in astonishment. The fire had been lit in a circle, and men were dancing in a fever of excitement. It was a corroboree. Possum skin rugs had been rolled up into tight bundles and the women were striking them with sticks and boomerangs, while the men danced in the firelight to the rhythm of the drums and the high-pitched chanting of the women.

For a long time Bohrah lay watching, with his head resting on his front paws, and his hind legs gathered up under him, ready to make his escape quickly if anyone noticed him. The dancers whirled round until they were gyrating like sparks from the fire. The booming of the drums grew faster and louder.

The excitement began to affect Bohrah. His breath came more quickly, his paws twitched, the hairs rose on his back, and his heart began to beat to the rhythm of the drums. With a howl he sprang to his feet, dashed through the circle of fire, and joined in the dance. At first no one took any notice of him, but presently the women shouted, half in fear, half in admiration. His long tail swung from side to side. It was so amusing that the dancers stopped and began

to laugh, until presently Bohrah found himself alone.

The beating of the possum skin bundles never stopped, the women kept on chanting, the men clapped their hands and rolled on their backs, helpless with laughter, while Bohrah solemnly danced on four feet, then on two, supporting himself with his tail.

One of the men had an amusing thought. He picked up one of the possum skin rolls and tied it to his girdle so that it hung behind him like Bohrah's tail. He put his elbows against his sides, with his hands dangling in front of him like paws, and hopped after the dancing Kangaroo. Others joined him, and soon there was a circle of men taking part in the Kangaroo Dance.

It went on until the darkness began to pale. In the chill morning air the older men of the tribe went to one side, and debated together gravely.

"Bohrah must be put to death," one said. "He has joined in the sacred corroboree and has learned things that should be hidden from animals. There is only one fate for an animal that has become as a man."

Another disagreed.

"We have learned something this night from Bohrah," he said. "He has taught us a new dance, the Dance of the Kangaroo. It is a time for rewarding rather than punishing."

The matter was debated at length.

"Bohrah has become one of us," it was decided. "From now on he will always walk or run or jump on two feet, like a man, and balance with his tail. We will leap as he has leaped, and in our corroborees we will dance as he has danced. He will be initiated into the tribe of Man, and he will be a Totem for us."

The men took Bohrah away from the women. They held him down on the ground and, with a stone for a mallet and a hard-pointed stick for a punch, they knocked out his front teeth in the rite that is performed when boys become men.

Then they set him free, and Bohrah hopped back to his feeding ground, leaping on his back legs, and supported by his tail. And so the Kangaroo Dance was born.

KOALA AND BUNYIP

WHO could ever imagine that the little Native Bear would ever have made friends with the cold, repellent monster of the swamps which the aborigine calls the Bunyip? But look closer and you will see strange markings in its fur. See how tightly its baby clings to its back. You may think that these things add to its quaintness, and show its lovable nature, but that is because you do not know how a single Koala once endangered a whole tribe.

The little Bear lived on the top of a mountain. Every night she came down to drink, and there she met the Bunyip who lived in the deepest, dreariest part of the swamp. Koala was not afraid of Bunyip. She was a cheerful little fellow.

"Hullo," she said when she first saw the Bunyip. "I thought you were part of the mountain, but when you moved I knew that you must be a Creature like myself. What are you doing here?"

Bunyip did not answer Koala's question, but asked, "Where do you come from, little Bear? I have never seen you before."

"I come down from my home every night to drink water. Would you like to come and see where I live?"

"Anything for a change from

this awful swamp," Bunyip said in a hollow voice, and he followed Koala up the steep mountain side. Trees snapped under his heavy tread, and large boulders crashed through the scrub. He sank down exhausted while Koala danced round him excitedly.

"It is the first time that a Koala has ever been visited by a Bunyip," she said. "We must celebrate the occasion, and she offered him delicacies from her food store. They disappeared quickly into Bunyip's capacious maw. His mouth split open in a cavernous grin, and the two animals talked together until the eastern sky paled. As the sun rose Bunyip lumbered down the mountain side and hid in the swamp.

It became a nightly occurrence, and the strangely assorted pair became firm friends. The other Koalas were uneasy and remonstrated with the Koala who lived on the mountain top.

"It is not right to be friendly with a horrible Bunyip," they said.

"Why not?" Mountain-top Koala asked truculently.

"We'll tell you why. We are all friends of Man, but Man is afraid of Bunyip. If he finds that one of us is fraternising with him he will hate us instead of loving us."

"Why do we want Man to love us? I don't care whether he loves me or whether he hates me."

"But we do! Man hunts Wallabies, and Kangaroos, and Wombats, and Lizards, and eats them, but he loves Koalas. If he hated us he would want to eat us too."

"You'd better be careful, then," Mountain-top Koala laughed, and raced away to meet her friend Bunyip.

The other bears continued their discussion.

"We will have to do something to bring her to her senses before it is too late," they said. "Let us see if we can learn anything from Man himself."

They crept away and climbed quietly into the branches of the trees round the camp site of Man. It was evening, and they could not be seen among the leaves, but they kept their eyes nearly closed so that they would not gleam in the firelight.

Soon the medicine man came into the circle of Men who were squatting on their haunches. He was painted with stripes of white and yellow clay to which tufts of cotton were clinging. He danced round the circle, waving his spear and using words that the Koalas could not understand.

In the morning they looked at each other sleepily.

"The magic is in the markings on his body," one of them said. "You must help me to put clay on my body in the same patterns, and then the Spirit of Man will come to our aid."

Before dusk the strangely marked Bear went up the mountain and found a little Koala waiting for its mother to return with Bunyip. Painted Koala picked it up and held it in his arms until a rumbling sound told him that the mother was coming home with her Bunyip friend. As soon as she appeared he put the baby firmly on her back and whispered in its ear, "Hang on tight. Never let go."

The magic in the taboo markings was so effective that the baby hung tightly to its mother. Every effort she made to dislodge it failed. Bunyip grew tired of waiting while Mountain-top Koala tried to get rid of her offspring. He had been hoping for a good meal and pleasant, dreamy conversation. After a while he got to his feet and went back to the swamp in disgust.

Painted Koala faced Mountain-top Koala.

"I am doing this for your own good as well as for the benefit of all our people," he said. "You will not easily get rid of your baby. To show how important this lesson really is, the marks that have been painted on me will always remain on the faces of our people, and on the fur of their heads."

He turned and ran back to his people and, as he had said, Mother Koala could not get rid of her baby, nor could she wash out the strange coloured marks that had appeared there while Painted Koala had been speaking. They are a reminder to every generation of Koalas that, if they value their lives, they must not associate with Bunyips.

KULAI AND CULMA

KULAI lived in the far north on the shore of the Gulf of Carpentaria. He was very young, so young that he could not be trusted far from his parents, who kept him safely hidden from their enemies in the bush.

Kulai was an adventurous young Echidna. While his mother and father were busy hunting food one day he scuttled off on his short little legs until he was out of sight. It was a lazy walkabout through the bush, but at last he came to a place where the trees were scattered and then stopped altogether. Kulai found himself looking out over waves of sand. He plodded on, over the ridges and into the valleys, his feet sinking deep into the sand. He came to the last ridge, and drew back in surprise. An endless sheet of blue water covered with white-capped waves stretched as far as the horizon. Kulai looked down and saw tiny little waves lapping against the sand.

He slipped down the steep slope and paddled in the cool water, laughing as the restless sand tickled his toes. Suddenly he squealed and jumped in alarm as a silver-white shape glided up to him.

"Who are you?" the silver-white thing asked.

"I am Kulai. Who are you?"

"I am Culma. I live in the water. Come with me where we can swim together in the deep sea, Kulai."

"No," said Kulai. "No. I have never seen so much water before. I am afraid."

"Oh, come on. I know you are a creature of the bush, but it is not an exciting place like the sea. The sea is an adventure, Kulai."

Adventure certainly appealed to Kulai. He waded in farther until he could no longer touch the sand with his feet.

"Farther, farther!" urged Culma.

Kulai was frightened. The little laughing waves slapped his face. He opened his mouth to cry, and his mouth and nose were filled with salt, stinging water. He spluttered and splashed frantically with his legs.

Culma swam up to him and said, "Now you are at my mercy, little Kulai. This is the moment I have been waiting for."

He opened his mouth wide. Kulai shrank into a ball and Culma swallowed him in one enormous gulp; and that was the end of little Kulai.

It was nearly the end of Culma, too. The spines of the Echidna stuck out and pierced his body. That is why Culma has a spiny fin and tail and is no longer smooth and shining as he was before he met Kulai the Echidna.

THE LAST SONG OF PRIEPRIGGIE

THE men were shuffling round in a circle, the sticks beating rhythmically and the song rising and falling in a cadence that followed the swaying bodies. It was a song to stir the blood, a dance to set the body quivering in an ecstasy that was partly poetry of motion and partly a wild abandon that made man one with nature, that gave him the zooming flight of the bees, the mile-long hopping of the kangaroo, the stir of sap in the trees in spring, that wedded him to earth as the Bandicoot and the Wombat are part of the earth. It was a song of Priepriggie, a song and dance that only Priepriggie could make out of the thoughts in his mind and the blood that pumped through his body.

It was in the Dreamtime, and only the combination of earth while it was young and the travail of earth as it laboured and brought new wonders to birth could ever have made a man such as Priepriggie.

"Let us honour Priepriggie in our corroboree," the men of the Dreamtime said. "Priepriggie is the song. Priepriggie is the dance. In the corroboree that Priepriggie has made, we are all Priepriggie."

And Priepriggie was in the song and the dance that he had made. He danced and he sang, and when the stars paled, he sank exhausted on the churned up sand. He lay on his back and looked at the stars that shone faintly on the brightening curtain of the sky and shouted, "Why don't you dance, stars? Why do you sit there silent and alone? Why don't you dance with us?"

It was light enough now for the men to see each others' eyes. They looked from one to another and saw the spark of laughter deep in the dark eyes beneath the overhanging brows. They whispered, "Priepriggie will make them dance and sing!"

But Priepriggie shrugged his shoulders and said, "It is enough if I make you dance. There's the big flying fox in the tree down by the river. I'll make him dance."

"It's getting late, Priepriggie. You'll never catch him now."

"Yes I will," Priepriggie boasted. "It's still dark where

the trees overhang the river. Come and see."

They crept after him like shadows and sank into the shade of the bushes, watching Priepriggie stealing towards the huge tree where all the flying foxes nested at night. He placed the butt of his spear in the notch in his woomera, drew back his arm, and sent the weapon between the branches like a flash of light.

A squeal of pain was drowned by the thrashing of wings as a thousand flying foxes woke and fled from the tree. They whirled in a circle watching as the spear fell from one branch to another, balanced for a moment, and fell to the ground. The body of the biggest flying fox lay still, with the shaft of Priepriggie's spear protruding from its chest and back and the blood dripping to the ground.

"Here is my meal, flying foxes," Priepriggie shouted. "Now you may dance and sing as your leader has danced and sung."

Their squeaky voices were unlike the voices of men, but the circle of flying foxes gyrated round the tree, and the song of the corroboree was echoed by the weird chorus. The circle turned faster and came closer to the ground. Priepriggie staggered in the whirlwind caused by the beating of many wings. His feet left the ground. He turned round and round and was slowly carried out of sight of the men who had risen from their hiding places, holding their heads back until the noise of the wings died away and nothing was to be seen of the mighty flock of flying foxes and their friend Priepriggie.

"Look for his handiwork in the sky," said Priepriggie's wife; but though they looked everywhere the man and the flying foxes had disappeared.

After the hot day the night air was cold and frosty. The bewildered men huddled together, longing for Priepriggie to lead them in the dance.

"Listen men!" his wife called to them. "Listen! It is Priepriggie!"

From far away they heard the voice of their friend chanting. They shuffled their feet in the dust and began to move round, their bodies undulating in time to the music. They joined in with the distant song. They lost all sense of time and space until the woman's voice cut through the song just as Priepriggie's spear had plunged through the body of the flying fox.

"Look up! Look up, men! The stars are dancing!"

They stopped and looked up. The stars were twinkling in the frosty night air and dancing together. Never had so many stars been seen together at one time before. They were clustered so thickly together that they shed a light—the broad band of light that men now call Warrambool, the Milky Way. They were singing Priepriggie's last song and dancing his last dance.

LAUGHING JACKASS AND THE SUN FIRE

THERE was a time when the only light in the world came from the moon and stars. Even when the moon was full and sailed across the sky like a gigantic silver ball, black shadows lurked under the trees. When the moon was a small sliver of light, the huge animals who lived before man was born could only grope their way through the gloom. And when clouds covered the sky, or when there was no moon, the world was still and every living thing slept. It was but a shadow world, gloomy and mysterious, where birds and animals fought constantly amongst themselves.

Under a cloudy, moonless sky, Dinewan the Emu and Brolga the Native Companion were fighting. There was no purpose in their quarrel, but they tried to kill each other. Dinewan sent the smaller bird head over heels in the sand and raked his body with strong claws. Brolga struggled to his feet and ran to Emu's nest. He picked up the largest of the eggs and with a quick jerk of his beak tossed it into the air.

Instead of rising in a curve and falling back, the egg went up until it reached the sky, where it smashed into a pile of firewood which the spirits had built. The egg broke, the yellow yoke flowed over the wood and burst into flame. The sky glowed in the light of the flames and, for the first time since the world was created, it glowed with colour. Warmth crept into the cold valleys, the lakes steamed gently, and all the animals basked in the unaccustomed heat.

The sky spirits were entranced with the beauty of the world that was revealed to them, and they agreed to light such a fire every day. During the hours of darkness each night they gathered firewood ready for the morning. To their surprise the animals often continued to sleep after the light flooded the world.

"They need to be told, so that they will be ready to see the fire as soon as it is lit," they decided, and they hung a bright morning star as a sign that the fire would soon be kindled.

But still the lazy animals slept on.

"Light is evidently not enough," they said. "We need someone to make a noise that will wake them up," and even as they spoke they heard a merry voice that rang out from the trees far below.

"Goor-gour-gaga! Goor-gour-gaga!"

"That is Goor-gour-gaga," they exclaimed. "He can do just what we want!"

They flew down and found him sitting on a branch, laughing and chattering.

"Goor-gour-gaga!" they said, "we want you to help us."

Laughing Jackass chattered with his bill, and then sat and listened.

"Do you like the big fire we light every morning? The fire that gives warmth and light, and which we call the sun?"

"I do—Goor-gour-gaga, Goor-gour-gaga," he replied. "But what has that got to do with me?"

"All you have to do is to laugh, just as you were doing then," they told him. "We want you to wake up when the evening star grows pale. That is when we light the fire. There is only a tiny flame at first, so small you can hardly see it—but you are clever, Goor-gour-gaga."

Jackass puffed out his chest and agreed with them.

"If you laugh, you will wake every one up, and they will be ready for the work of another day."

"And if I won't do it?"

They looked at him sorrowfully.

"Then we will not light the fire, and the world will be dark and cold as it has always been. It will be the same for you as for all the other birds and animals, Goor-gour-gaga."

The bird startled them with an ear-splitting shriek of laughter.

"Like that?" he asked.

"Yes, yes, just like that, Goor-gour-gaga."

"Of course I will do it. I like to hear my own voice as much as you do."

They hid their smiles, and commended him. "But remember, if you do not laugh at dawn, we will not light the sun fire."

Every day begins with Goor-gour-gaga's laughter. The fire of the sun is kindled by the spirits of the sky, and as the wood catches fire, the flames grow higher. By midday the blaze is at its fiercest, but during the afternoon it dies down, and when evening comes, only the embers remain. They glow hotly, and their red gleam is often seen after sunset. A few of the embers are saved by the sky spirits, who wrap them in fleecy layers of cloud and keep them alive ready to light the fire the following morning . . . the morning which the Laughing Jackass will herald with his raucous, exuberant cry of

"Goor-gour-gaga!"

THE MISERABLE MOPOKE

THERE was a bad-tempered man who was so surly, and who disliked other people's company so much that he went away to live by himself. He was frightened that if he stayed with the tribe he would be expected to help with all kinds of jobs. When by himself he had plenty of time to do the things he wanted. After he had lived alone for some years he had a magnificent collection of spears, boomerangs, nulla-nullas, and kangaroo and possum skin rugs. The name of this

man was Mooregoo, the Mo-
poke.

One night Bahloo, the Moon,
came down to earth. He was
cold and hungry, and walked
for a long way without finding
anywhere to shelter. Presently
he saw a gleam of firelight in
the distance. It was Mooregoo's
camp fire. Bahloo hurried towards it.

"Will you give me some-
thing to eat, please?" he asked
Mooregoo.

"No," said the solitary man
grumpily. "I have only enough
food for myself."

"Well, at least you can let
me warm myself by your fire."

"There is only enough fire
for me."

"But you have some fine
rugs. If you won't let me stay
by the fire, I will wrap myself
up in one of them."

"You leave the rugs alone,"
Mooregoo shouted. "I made
them for myself, not for idle
fellows who are not prepared to
help themselves."

Bahloo turned away and
went over to a tall gum tree.
Mooregoo looked at him
curiously as he took his flint
knife and cut a notch in the
trunk of the tree, and then
another a little higher up.
One after the other Bahloo cut

the notches in the tree trunk
and used them as steps to
climb up to the first branches.
He did not stay there, but went
on until he came to a comfortable fork where two
branches met. Still using his
knife, he stripped a large piece
of bark from the tree and
covered himself with it.

By this time the sun had
risen. Bahloo chanted incantations and muttered magic
spells. The wind came up,
driving the heavy clouds before
it, until the sun was covered.
Then the rain began to fall.
Mooregoo took shelter in his
humpy, but before long the
river began to rise and covered
the whole of his camping
ground. It swirled between the
trees and washed away his
spears and nullanullas and
boomerangs and his precious
skin rugs. Then it surged
round the humpy and washed
that away too.

Mooregoo rushed from one
tree to another, trying to
climb up the smooth trunk,
but he could not find a foothold. The waters rose higher
still, and he was carried away
in the flood.

Bahloo smiled grimly as he
heard the man's voice dying
away in the distance. Mooregoo

was changed into a Mopoke, but he still cries with a mournful voice. When the blackfellows hear it, they say to their friends, "Don't be a Mopoke,"

because they remember what happened to bad-tempered, surly Mooregoo in the days when Bahloo came down to earth.

THE MOON'S REWARD

Two brothers were looking for honey. Their search led them a long distance, but at last they found a bees' nest in a hollow tree. The bees were flying in and out of a hole in the trunk several feet from the ground.

"There will be a fine supply of honey here," one of the brothers said. "No one has been here before. Put your hand inside and pull it out."

"No," his brother replied. "Your arms are longer than mine. You pull it out."

"My skin is not as hard as yours. I would get badly stung."

"And what about me? Do you think the bees will leave me alone? Anyway, you are the oldest. It is only right that you should show me how to get the honey out of the tree."

"Yes, I am older than you, and as you are the younger brother, I tell you to get it. If you don't I'll set about you with my club, and then you can tell me whether bee stings

are worse than waddy blows."

The younger brother gave way and gingerly thrust his hand into the hole, blocking it completely. The bees were puzzled. They buzzed round trying to find an entrance, but made no attempt to sting the honey thief.

"I can't feel any honey," he said. "Only bees crawling over my fingers."

"Put your arm right in, man," his brother urged. "The honey is sure to be farther down the trunk."

The young man pressed hard against the bole of the tree and thrust his arm down to its fullest extent.

"I can just touch the honey," he exclaimed. "It is sticky on my fingers,"

"Then pull it out!"

"I can't. I can touch it, but I can't get my fingers round it. It's too far down."

"Oh, you are a fool. Why didn't I do it myself!"

"Because you were frightened of the bees, elder brother.

Now you know that they won't hurt you, perhaps you would like to try for yourself."

He began to pull his arm out of the hole. It had been a very tight squeeze getting it in, but by now his arm was swollen and covered with honey."

"I can't get it out," he complained. "My elbow is stuck and it hurts."

His brother caught hold of his other arm and began to pull.

"Stop! Stop!" the young man shouted. "You're hurting!"

"It'll hurt more before I'm finished with you. I can't leave you like this, and anyway I want my honey."

He began to jerk savagely, holding on to his brother's arm with both hands and pressing his feet against the trunk of the tree.

The young brother, who was little more than a boy, began to scream with pain. The elder brother let go and sat down to think.

"I will get other people to help. If we all pull at once we'll have your arm out before you know where you are."

"No, no," pleaded the other. "I think you have broken it already. You'll have to find some other way."

"Very well. I'll go and get help. There may be some wise man who can tell us a better way to free you."

There were a number of hunters on the plain. He ran swiftly from one to another, telling them what had happened, and begging them to help, but they were too intent on their tasks and refused abruptly. Some said they were sorry and would come later, others were angry and drove him away because he was frightening the game, and some thought it was all a huge joke. The only one who could help was a round-faced man named Moon.

"Where is he?" asked Moon. "I think I know what to do. Take me to him."

When they got to the tree the poor young man was dangling helplessly by his arm and almost unconscious. Moon climbed nimbly into the branches of the tree and found the hollow shaft below him. He put his head right inside and gave a tremendous sneeze. The imprisoned arm was blown out of the hole, followed by a cloud of angry bees and a large quantity of honey.

The three men sat down to eat. The two brothers were angry because the other hunters had refused to help, and they plotted vengeance.

"The wind is blowing towards them, and there is a lot of dry grass about," the younger brother suggested.

"Don't do it," Moon begged. "You may find yourselves in trouble if you try to burn them up."

"We won't do that," elder brother said, rubbing the hard edge of his woomera on a dry log. "We'll smoke them out and drive the game farther away."

A wisp of smoke came from the log. He blew the tinder and fed the tiny flame with wisps of grass until the wind fanned it

to a blaze. The fire spread quickly, but the wind shifted and started to blow towards them. The three men turned and ran, but the fire gained on them. Moon stumbled and fell flat on his face.

"He helped us, now we must help him," younger brother gasped.

The brothers turned to Moon, seized an arm and a foot on either side, and swung him backwards and forwards, higher and higher. When they released him he shot up into the sky.

The brothers kept on running until they were lost to sight, even to Moon, who liked his new home in the sky so much that he has remained there ever since.

THE OYSTER BROTHERS AND THE SHARK

THE Oyster brothers sat on the beach watching Shark as he rushed backwards and forwards. It was a beautiful day with a cloudless sky and a soft, cool breeze blowing along the beach. They had full bellies and nothing to do but watch Shark chasing the stingrays. Presently he caught one and carried it to the beach, where he left it on the sand and went back to hunt for more.

"It would make a good meal for us when we feel hungry again," one of the Oyster brothers remarked.

"Yes, much better to eat when someone else has caught it! Let's hide it."

They carried the stingray to their camp in the scrub on the edge of the beach and covered it with branches and wisps of dried grass.

Shark had no more luck

after his one catch. The sting-rays had decided that the stretch of open water was no place for them when Shark was on the prowl, and had gone to a bay where they could hide among the rocks.

Shark waded out of the water and looked everywhere for his stingray. He noticed the Oyster brothers who were sitting innocently on the sand. He strode up to them.

"Where is my stingray?" he demanded.

"What stingray?"

"You know very well. I left it here a while ago, and you are the only people on the beach."

The elder Oyster held out his hands as if to show that they were empty.

"We have been here all day and we haven't seen any sting-rays. They don't go walking about on the beach for our benefit, you know."

Shark made an angry noise and stalked away. As he was leaving he turned and said threateningly, "If it was you who took it, you will be sorry."

After giving him plenty of time to get away, elder Oyster stood up and said to his brother, "Do you feel like a nice feed of stingray?"

"Yes, that would be good,

but where can we find one?"

"Who knows?" elder brother chuckled. "Maybe the good spirits have left one in our camp. Let's go and see."

"There you are!" big brother Oyster said as he pulled it out from under the leaves and grass. "It's a pity Shark isn't here. He could have shared it with us."

Some time later he wiped his mouth and patted his stomach.

"But perhaps it's just as well," he remarked. "There was only enough for us."

They lay down by the fire to sleep; and then it was morning, and Shark was kicking them.

"You have been eating sting-ray," he shouted. "I knew you had stolen mine."

"How can you be sure?" the elder Oyster asked. "Ouch! Stop it! That hurt. How do you know it was your stingray? We are able to go fishing just as well as you are."

Shark towered over him.

"Oysters are too lazy to go fishing for themselves. I know you are the thieves."

He belaboured young brother Oyster with his spear, and when elder brother Oyster tried to protect him he pushed him aside. He drew back his spear ready to hurl it at him. Oyster struck it aside with his woomera and leaped on to Shark, who grappled with him at once. They fell to the ground, rolling over the ashes of the dead fire. Shark managed to struggle to his feet. He buried his hands in the ashes, smearing them over Oyster's body until he was covered with the white powder. Stung to retaliation, Oyster dug out some hot sand and threw it into Shark's eyes, until he begged for mercy.

The Oyster brothers stood back, but Shark was not finished with them. Swinging his waddy round his head, he brought it down twice, flattening the bodies of the Oysters. The younger one was so furious with pain that he chased Shark down the beach and into the water, where he flung his boomerang at him. It stuck into his back, projecting above the water as Shark swam out to sea.

None of them forgot that day. Shark's eyes have been small ever since because of the

hot sand that was thrown into them, and Oyster's boomerang is still in his back. As for the Oysters, they were so small and flat after their beating, and covered with white ashes, that they crept round to the hiding place of the stingrays and sank down into the water, where they attached themselves to the rocks and waited for someone to come and eat them. And someone always does!

RAINBOW INTO FISH INTO MOUNTAIN

RAINBOW bent over the pool and looked at the woman who was stooping to gather the roots of the water lilies. She was as graceful as a bird with the water glistening on her skin and her long arms weaving through the clear water.

Rainbow had never seen such a beautiful sight in all his life, and he was on fire with love.

He slid silently into the water and changed himself into a fish. He swam towards her, his heart beating quickly at the sight of her legs and body and the arms that stretched down to the bed of the lagoon, and disappeared as the woman rose to put the roots in her dilly bag. He tried to rub his body against her legs, but she had finished her work and was climbing on to the bank. Rainbow-Fish looked up at her. She was conscious of the eyes that peered so intently at her from the water. Her teeth showed in a smile as she lifted her yam stick and tried to use it as a spear. She could not touch the fish. She struck at it as though the digging stick were a waddy, but she only splashed the water until it sparkled like a fountain in the sunlight.

The smile faded from her face. The fish was growing bigger. Its sides swelled like the moon, and it grew bigger and longer.

"A bunyip!" the woman gasped and turned to run, but she slipped on the wet grass. She heard the fish scrambling out of the water and felt it slide under her body until she was sitting astride its back. The fish soared into the air and carried the helpless woman far across the plain. It flew over her own camp site and she caught a glimpse of her husband staring up at her with his mouth open wide in amazement.

For many miles she travelled on the back of the flying fish, but at length it grew tired; it sank down and turned into a mountain rock.

Presently a man came loping across the plain. It was the husband, who had noted the direction taken by the fish. When he saw his wife, her waist was still encircled by an arm of stone. He attacked the rock fiercely with his nulla-nulla. The fish that had once been a rainbow had now taken the shape of a man. With single blow the husband half severed the man-mountain's neck. The stone arm relaxed and the woman fled towards her husband, but she was destined not to reach him.

A flash of light which contained all the colours of the rainbow enveloped the rock. It grew as quickly as it had done when it was a fish, but now the growth continued un-checked. The rock swelled and split and towered up towards the sky in the form of a mountain. All the power of the Rainbow was concentrated in that gleaming, coruscating light. A streamer of many-coloured flame reached out and touched the man and the woman, turning them into stone pillars. Rainbow-Mountain lost his strength in that last manifestation of power. He never stirred again, his feet buried deep in the desert sand, while close by him the pillars of stone turn to each other as if in fear of the mountain that broods throughout eternity on the memory of unfulfilled love.

THE RAINBOW SNAKE

THE two boys had been chosen to accompany the men when they left on their long journey to the sea to catch fish. The boys had never been away from the inland hunting grounds before. The crossing of the mountains, through the densely bushed valleys, and over the bare pass where the clouds settled in a heavy mist, had been filled with new and exciting experiences.

Camp was made in a sheltered valley. The boys were up early the next morning. They fanned the embers of the camp fire into a blaze and heated stones ready for the morning meal, but their hopes were dashed to the ground when the elders told them that they must stay in camp.

"But we wanted to come with you for the fishing," they said. "We have never seen the ocean."

"You must be patient and wait until you are older," they were told. "We are going to leave our food and weapons here, and someone must stay in camp to look after them."

The boys concealed their disappointment and pretended to be proud of the responsibility that had been given to them.

"Perhaps we could go down for a little while . . . just to watch," one of them said. "We could go one at a time so that the camp would not be left unguarded."

"You will both stay here all the time," the leader said sternly. "Do not leave the camp. If you go into the bush you may be attacked by wild dogs. If you go to the beach you would be in danger from Thugine, the great snake that lives in the sea."

The boy was about to say something, but he changed his mind. As soon as the men had gone and their voices had died away, he turned to his friend and said, "I don't believe what they say about Thugine. Snakes don't live in the sea. It's only a tale to scare us so that we won't follow them. I'm going down soon. We didn't come all this way to be scared by a yarn that only women would believe."

"I'll come with you," his friend said. "I'm not going to stay here alone."

They waited for a while and then went stealthily through the trees, which thinned out as they came close to the seashore. They stopped and stared at the sight that met their eyes. The sand was white, and as far as they could see the white waves hissed across the flat, wet beach. Farther out the sea was a deeper blue than the sky, and white waves curled over it. Seagulls wheeled overhead, their mournful cries blending with the song of the waves. Far away they could see the little black dots which were the men of their tribe.

"Come on!" the older boy shouted. They raced down to the water and plunged in, shrieking with delight as they were tumbled about by the waves. Before they realised what was happening they were caught by the undertow and swept out of their depth. Cloud shadows raced across the water, and below them another shadow, long, sinuous, menacing, followed them. It was Thugine. He wrapped his body round the struggling boys and dragged them to his lair beneath the waves.

In the late afternoon the men returned to camp, burdened with their catch. Nothing had been disturbed, but there was no sign of the boys. The men shouted and searched. Darkness fell and the search was abandoned, but early the following morning they trailed the boys down to the beach. The footsteps led to the water and were lost to sight.

"They have been taken by Thugine," the leader said. "I warned them against him, but they disobeyed my orders."

He looked out to sea. Two rocks projected above the water, their sides lashed by the waves. "There they are," he said sadly. "Thugine has turned them into barren islands. And there is Thugine himself!"

A brilliant bow was arched across the sky, embracing both rocky islands. If sometimes you see it for yourself, you will know that Thugine is the Rainbow Snake who lives in the sea and who sometimes arches his multi-coloured body far into the sky.

THE RAINBOW SNAKES

FAR away in the Northern Territory, in a river that flows into the Gulf of Carpentaria, live the Rainbow Snake and his wife. Rainbow Snake is the guardian of the river. He allows the black people to catch fish when they are hungry, but if they spear them for fun, he becomes very angry.

Rainbow Snake is a beautiful creature, with long red and yellow stripes down his body. His wife is blue from the top of her head to the tip of her tail. After a shower of rain they sometimes stroll together, and their bodies can be seen in a huge curve that stretches across the sky. It is then that the blackfellow must be careful, because Rainbow Snake can dart down like lightning to pick up anyone who has been foolish enough to catch fish for sport. As a just retribution he feeds them to the fish in the river.

A long time ago a shower of hailstones fell near the river. The oldest people in the tribe have never seen anything like these white stones before. As soon as the stinging shower was over they rushed outside their gunyahs and looked at them for a long time. The hailstones did not move, but slowly, ever so slowly, they seemed to burrow into the ground, and disappeared. There was much argument as to whether they had simply grown small and vanished, or whether they had made their way into the ground.

"They must still be there," one of the elders said emphatically. "Give me a yam stick."

One of the women handed him her digging stick, and he turned over the ground in several places. At the bottom of the holes he found worms, which was not really surprising, for if you dig in the right place you will nearly always find worms.

"These are the children of the Rainbow Snake," the old men said triumphantly. "They have hatched out of the white eggs that fell from the sky."

And because it was the oldest, wisest man in the tribe who said it, everyone has known, ever since that day, that hailstones are the eggs of the Rainbow Snake and his wife.

THE REBELLIOUS SON OF BAIAME

In the Barwon River there is a large pool called Wirreebilla; and nearby there is a tree with a lump on the bark which is known to the tribes for hundreds of miles around as the Goodoo of Wirreebilla. This is the story of Goodoo.

Long ago Baiame and one of his sons were fishing at the pool. They caught an enormous Goodoo, or Codfish. It was so large that it was a struggle to get it ashore. When it was safely landed, Baiame cut two large slices of its flesh which he put on the fire that his son had kindled. The remainder of the fish was hung on the bough of a tree.

There was a tempting aroma as the fish was cooked. Baiame took it out of the fire and sank his teeth into one of the slices. His son put out his hand to take the other piece, but Baiame struck it away. With starting eyes the young man watched his father eat the first slice and make a start on the second. He flung down the bank in a temper and, hidden from his father, wrought magic spells that caused the water to whirl round faster and faster until it surged down the river, carrying all the fish with it. As the torrent flooded the river from bank to bank, the boy ran alongside it, laughing as he saw the fish swept helplessly along.

Baiame finished his meal, wiped his hands, and called

his son. There was no answer. He called again, and then walked over to the pool. There was only a little muddy water at the bottom, and he knew at once what had happened. He strode down the river in a temper. He could see the traces of the flood-water, but mile after mile went by without any sign of his son. Then, far in the distance, he caught sight of him.

"Stop!" he called.

His son kept on running. Baiame gave a slow smile. He knew that where his son was going the river plunged underground. When the boy halted, he came closer and said, "You wanted to go with the river. Go on. Go on under the earth and never let me see you again."

The boy was defiant. He had never stood up to his father's anger before, but he was so resentful of Baiame's selfishness that he shouted, "Be quiet, old man. Turn into stone."

The veins stood out on Baiame's forehead, and his face turned almost black with rage. He threw out his arms, and his son was forced back, step by step, until he fell into the river and was swept underground.

The great wirrinun walked slowly away. He never saw his son again, but the curse lingered over him all his life. In his home in the sky he stands, partly turned to stone because of the words that his son uttered before he was buried in the underground river.

And the Goodoo of Wirreebilla remains as a sign that the great evil of other days really happened.

THE RED CLOUD

INETINA walked along the reef looking into the clear water to see if he could find any edible fish. He poked his spear into the crevices between the brilliant masses of coral, but the only fish he disturbed were poisonous varieties or those that were unfit to eat. An open clam attracted his attention. He jabbed the spear points at it petulantly before going on to the next pool. Behind his back the water swirled as the clam surged along to the next pool that the fisherman was approaching. Inetina was unaware of what was happening until he found himself staring into the gaping jaws of the shellfish which lay across his path.

He fell back a pace. The spear dropped out of his hand when he saw a black face inside the shell, and two eyes that glared at him.

"Who are you?" the apparition demanded. "What is your name?"

"I am Inetina."

"What are you doing here?"

"I have come to spear fish. Is it any affair of yours?" Inetina asked, his self-possession returning.

"That is not my affair, but the fact that you speared me in my home is very much my affair."

Inetina then realised that there was an ugly wound in the face, from which the blood poured down and dripped into the water, forming a dusky red cloud which obscured the colours of the coral.

"I am sorry. I did not mean to hurt you."

"If you were a man you would have known what you were doing. You act like a woman. I don't believe you are a man at all."

Inetina thrust out his jaw at the insult. Exerting all his strength, he snapped off a huge mass of coral and hurled it at the human clam so forcibly that the shellfish was swept into the pool and crushed.

Blood seeped out of the broken shell, turning the pink water a deep red. It rose to the surface and emerged as a red mist which enveloped the fisherman and was blown by the sea breeze towards the land. It spread across the coast until only the tops of the tallest trees showed above it. Farther and farther the cloud spread until at last it was stopped by the inland mountain wall.

Everything in the cloud died —insects and birds, animals and men, and silence fell over the land. Only two people survived, a brother and sister who were fleet-footed, and were able to reach the nearest mountain and climb its steep sides until they were far above the cloud.

They waited there many days until the cloud thinned and was blown away. Hand in hand they descended to the plain and wandered south until they came to a land where they could hear the cheerful voices of birds once more, and found grubs and animals which provided them with food.

It is a forbidden thing for

brother and sister to marry and have children, but in the dead of night a spirit spoke to them.

"Death came to your tribe because of the evil deed of Inetina; but it is not right that the thoughtlessness of one man should cause a whole tribe to die. You are the hope of those who lived and now are dead."

"What can we do?"

"You must marry and have children."

"But we are brother and sister!"

"The gods have given their consent, for in you and in you alone lives the future of your tribe."

Then the two young people turned and embraced each other; and from their union came that strong and powerful

tribe, the Udwadja, who will occupy the land and live for ever.

ROLLA-MANO AND THE STARS

DARK brown and green foliage waved lazily in front of Rolla-mano's cave home. The light was dim when he came out carrying his spears and net and pushed his way between the plants. Sand swirled round his feet and dropped slowly back, crabs scuttled out of the way, and a shoal of brightly-coloured fish darted round him like birds.

Rolla-mano was a man of the sea, and his house lay far beneath the surface of the water. The sand rose in front of him in a long slope, flattened out, and became muddy with the silt brought down by the river. Presently his head and body rose above the water. Breathing the salty air of the mangrove swamp as easily as the denser sea water, Rolla-mano threw his net. It settled in a circle and sank down, imprisoning a number of fish. He carried them in the net as though it were a bag, climbed out of the swamp, and put them on the ground. Swiftly he gathered dry moss and sticks, and soon had a fire going. He was ready to cook the fish when he heard voices in the distance.

He picked up a flaming brand, stamped out the fire, ran to where the mangrove trees grew thickly beside a faint path, and hid amongst them. Two young women strolled towards him. Rolla-mano's eyes gleamed like points of fire in the gathering darkness. As the young women came closer he could hear what they were saying.

"I tell you I saw a fire somewhere by the swamp," one of the girls said. "There is still a smell of wood smoke in the air."

"You are imagining things," the other laughed. "No one ever comes down to the mangrove swamp."

"I don't care. I know someone is here!"

She began to run down the path with her companion close behind her.

Rolla-mano swung the smouldering stick through the air and it burst into flame, lighting up the path. He jumped in front of the girls and sent his net outwards and upwards so that it began to settle over them. The first girl dived under it, ran down the path, screaming with fear, and jumped into the water. The man of the sea jerked the draw-string tight so that the second girl was caught in the net. He jumped on to the root of a tree which shone like a snake in the torch-light.

"There are crocodiles there," he called to the first girl. "Come back!"

The girl took no notice but struck out in the water in a frenzy of fear. Rolla-mano uttered an imprecation and jumped out as far as he could, intending to follow her. The moment the flaming branch touched the water it seemed to explode. The sparks flew in every direction and floated up into the sky, where they became stars. In the darkness Rolla-mano lost sight of the fugitive. He turned back, climbed ashore, and walked along the path until he came to the girl who was struggling on the ground trying to get rid of the net in which she was imprisoned.

The man of the sea stooped over her, feeling with his hands until he found the opening of the net. He stripped the clinging meshes off, held her until her trembling ceased and then, clasping her hands tightly in his, mounted up into the sky, following the sparks from his torch. He made a new home for himself there, forsaking the sea which was his natural element. The girl he changed into the evening star. Every night when the sky is clear of clouds she gazes from the vast, star-studded dome of night searching for the friend who would not heed her warning, but who, by her agility and presence of mind, escaped the clutches of the man of the sea.

THE SANDPIPER'S MISFORTUNE

PIPIPA the Sandpiper was making a spear. He had spent a long time trimming and polishing the shaft, chipping the head to a sharp edge, and binding it firmly to the shaft with gut. All that remained to be done was to coat the binding with melted gum.

He lit a fire and put a lump of red gum on a stone.

"As soon as I've finished I'll show it to my brothers the Carpet Snakes," he mused as he bent over the gum and poked it to see whether it was soft enough. A tongue of fire darted out and licked the gum. It burst into flame. Pieces of burning gum flew in all directions, some of them hitting Pipipa on the nose and legs and clinging there in spite of all his efforts to dislodge them.

"Help! Help!" he screamed.

Far away the Carpet Snakes heard him and turned to each other in alarm.

"It is our brother Pipipa!" they exclaimed.

They raced towards his camp and saw him writhing in agony.

"Look, he is covered with burning gum."

They tore it off.

"What have you been doing? Your legs are burnt to thin sticks and your nose is not like any nose we have ever seen. It is a beak! You have turned yourself into a bird!"

"Don't be silly," Pipipa snapped. "How could I know that the gum would explode?"

He looked down at his thin legs and felt his sharp, protruding nose. "Don't you feel sorry for me, my brothers?"

The tears rolled down their cheeks.

"We are truly sorry, Pipipa. Sorry because we laughed at you, but you did look funny and we couldn't help it. More sorry because you have hurt yourself and changed into a bird."

"I'm not a bird," Pipipa shouted angrily.

He beat his arms against his body, but was dismayed to find that they looked like wings.

His brothers lifted him up and carried him down to the beach. He struggled and kept on shouting, "Not a bird! Not a bird!"

"Poor fellow," they said, wagging their heads. "We'll make a good camp for him. It will be like a swamp with plenty of water and with fish for him to catch."

They dug a wide hole. The tide crept up the beach and filled it, making a large lagoon. Carpet Snakes laid their brother beside it and went back to their own camp.

When they were out of sight Sandpiper staggered to his feet and bent over to look at his reflection in the swamp water. He sighed and whispered, "Not a bird!" but in his heart he knew he was indeed a bird destined to spend its life in the swamps and lagoons by the seashore.

THE SCULPTOR

THERE was once a strange little boy who belonged to the Goola-willeel tribe. Some say that his name was Yagam, which is also the name of a famous leader, but we shall call him Goola-willeel, which means Topknot Pigeon. He had few friends and was not interested in playing with other children. There was nothing he liked better than to go away by himself and make tiny figures out of sticks and leaves, or to draw pictures in the sand. He made another world out of his pictures—a world that he could live in, where he could have adventures, a world that was much more exciting than the camp where he lived. The faces of his relatives were all familiar, and he knew their thoughts and what they were going to say before they opened their mouths. He was not interested in learning to play with spears, nor in tracking and hunting.

All he wanted was to be left alone and spend the day with the creatures he had made in his own private world.

But little boys cannot be allowed to go their own way. Each one is a member of his tribe, and the strength of a tribe lies in its hunters and warriors. Goola-willeel was taken away from the women-folk and went through the long initiation ceremonies. He proved that he could conquer appetite and pain and fear, and he became a man—but still he was not a hunter or a warrior.

His mother and sisters set out one morning with their digging sticks and passed Goola-willeel, who was sneaking off to his favourite hiding place among the trees.

"You are a man now, Goola-willeel," his mother said. "We expect you to provide a kangaroo for the evening meal while we gather the roots and grubs."

The young man sighed. He went back to the camp to get his spears and woomera, and set off to look for kangaroos. He did not find any. In fact he did not even look for their tracks. He wandered among the wattle trees gathering gum, until by the end of the day he had a small heap of it. He hid it carefully and returned home, where the women heaped abuse on him because he had brought no food with him.

Day after day passed in the same manner. The hidden pile of wattle gum grew larger, but at night, when he returned home empty-handed, he had to face the anger of the women.

One morning he went to his mother.

"Today I will bring back a kangaroo for you," he said.

"Not before time!" she retorted.

He hurried off to his pile of gum and spent the day fashioning it to the shape of a kangaroo. It was beautifully done. The face seemed alive. He stood back to admire it, lifted it carefully on to his shoulders, and carried it back. He put it on the ground and strolled over to the fire.

"Where is the kangaroo you promised us," his sister asked.

"Over there," he said. "I have carried it far enough. I am tired. You bring it in."

He squatted down, prepared to enjoy himself. His sister went over to it. She bent over the lifelike figure and then called to the other women.

"Come here and see what Goola-willeel has brought us!"

They ran to her, looked at the wattle-gum kangaroo in disgust, and returned to him.

The smile faded from the young man's face as he looked at them. There was no laughter in their eyes, no admiration, no appreciation of his delicate work of art. Instead there was a look that frightened him as they picked up their yam sticks and advanced menacingly towards him. He scrambled to his feet, but he was too late. They were on top of him, beating him with their sticks until he was covered with blood.

Never again was he allowed to go out hunting alone. He was always accompanied by other men, who watched him to see that he did not waste his time gathering wattle-gum.

And this is characteristic of all the Goola-willeels, the Topknot Pigeons, who fly in flocks in search of food, and never go out alone.

THE SHAMING OF RAINBOW SNAKE

At the bottom of the deep water hole Yurlunggur the Rainbow Snake raised his head and stirred uneasily. He could hear the unaccustomed sound of women's voices. The world still lay smooth and bare. The men who were to become animals had as yet been given no names, and no sound had ever disturbed the water hole at Mirramina until Misilgoe and Boalere came from the far south, naming plants and animals as they went.

Boalere threw herself on the ground. Far below, Yurlunggur's sensitive ears detected the vibrations. He listened and heard every word that was spoken.

"Sit down here, Misilgoe,

and rest while I cook a meal."

"Let me help you. You have caught the bandicoots and gathered the yams and lily bulbs. I can't let you do all the work."

Boalere smiled at her sister.

"Your baby will soon be born," she said. "It is time for you to rest."

She opened her dilly bag and shook the contents on to the ground. In addition to the flesh of the bandicoot and the bulbs there was a remnant of a wallaby they had eaten for their last meal, and a handful of witchetty grubs.

Boalere gathered dry grass and sticks, fossicking among the scrub and returning with her arms full of firewood. As she looked down at her sister the load fell on the ground and she gasped aloud. During her brief absence Misilgoe had given birth to her baby, who was cradled in her arms.

"My dear," Boalere cried, "you must eat. I will hurry."

She kindled a fire and in the gathering darkness groped for the food she had prepared. It was not there. Her dilly bag lay where she had put it, but the ground where the food had been emptied was bare. By the flickering light of the fire she saw a movement out of the

corner of her eye. The bandicoot had come to life and was running towards the water hole, followed by the wallaby which ran on the two legs that the sisters had left after their last meal. After the animals went a hurrying procession of witchetty grubs, arching their bodies and crawling towards the water. One by one they reached the bank and plunged into the pool, sinking down through the water and into the open mouth of Yurlunggur.

"Never mind," Misilgoe pacified her sister. "We will get more food in the morning. Let us tear the bark from one of these trees and make a cradle for my son."

The darkness deepened. It was suffused by a dim light which grew steadily as the moon rose behind the trees until everything was bathed in a cold, silvery glow. Misilgoe fell asleep with her hand resting on her baby's cradle, but Boalere could not shake off a feeling of apprehension. She glanced uneasily at the pool which lay black and silent under the shadow of the trees.

Something rose above the surface. The ripples spread outwards, flashing in the moonlight. The head of the snake rose menacingly in the night air. It swayed slowly backwards and forwards. Boalere scrambled to her feet, clutching two sticks in her trembling hands, and began to beat them together. Her voice rose, quavering at first, gathering strength as she sang the words of a song. Her feet moved faster and faster, and as she danced and sang, and beat time with the sticks, the snake lifted itself above the water, its head and body swaying rhythmically to the chant. Hour after hour the dance went on while Misilgoe and her baby slumbered peacefully.

The moon completed its journey across the sky and sank behind the western hills. As it disappeared the snake sank back into the pool and the ripples closed over its head. Boalere fell by the side of her sister and slept the sleep of exhaustion.

The head emerged again. The body of Yurlunggur slithered across the ground, its head weaving between the bushes, and hung over the cradle. It was puzzled by the tiny form. It sank its teeth into the baby's flesh. The cry woke the infant's mother and aunt, but before they could drive sleep away, Yurlunggur's mouth gaped wide and closed over them.

Yurlunggur lay on the ground for a long time unable to move, with two large bulges and a smaller one distending his body. Presently he wriggled uncomfortably. His head rose slowly upwards, reaching towards the sky. Loop after loop of his body uncoiled until only the tip of his tail was resting on the ground. The body arched through the sky, pulsating with changing colours. His tongue flickered in and out, flashing with blinding light, and when he spoke his voice was like thunder rolling round the hills.

"Listen, snakes!" he boomed. "I am Yurlunggur the Rainbow Snake. Come out of your holes and listen to me."

He looked down and saw the thin black threads as they crept out, and even the cold glint of their eyes.

"Two women came from the south land, and a small man thing that was born in the night."

"Where are they now?" The voices were thin in the morning air.

Yurlunggur's laugh boomed out.

"Dead!" he shouted. "Dead.

Dead. Entombed in my body. You see I have protected you, snakes. Women are evil. They would take the Dreamtime away from us."

"Shame on you, Yurlunggur!" the thin voices cried. "Shame, shame, shame!"

Yurlunggur lowered his head. It sped towards them like a meteor and hovered above the trees.

"Why is there shame?" it asked. "It was to protect you that I destroyed the evil ones, the women and their offspring."

"We cannot remain for ever in the Dreamtime, Yurlunggur. The women were not evil. It is you who has brought evil to our land."

There was a chorus of approval.

"Are you all against me?" Rainbow Snake asked.

Again a hissing chorus showed that all the snakes were in agreement.

Yurlunggur lowered himself. His mouth opened to its widest extent. With his body flat on the ground, he heaved. The women tumbled out of his mouth, and Misilgoe waited for her son who laughed and gurgled as he fell into the waiting arms.

Boalere and Misilgoe continued their leisurely progress through the northern territory, naming all the plants and animals, but Yurlunggur stayed at the bottom of the water hole and never showed himself again as the Rainbow Snake.

THE SON OF MOUNT GAMBIER

THE slopes of Mount Gambier are scarred and seamed with rifts caused by the tears she has shed over the evil wrought by her son Woo. Some say Gambier was a giantess who lived in the mountains, but others believe that the mountain is the goddess herself. She is ageless. Many centuries have passed since her grief manifested itself in the deeply-cut grooves in her sides.

Woo was her son in the days of her youth. He was a misshapen and amusing figure, but in spite of his grotesque appearance, his mother loved him. He was a tiny midget to be the son of such a gigantic mother. He was four feet in height, with only one arm which grew out of his chest, and one leg.

What he missed in appearance, he made up for in agility.

He had taught himself to walk by twisting his foot, heel and toe, and in this curious way he could cover twice the distance that an ordinary man could travel in a single day.

It is said that Woo was the friend of insects, lizards, and snakes. He hunted animals for food, and counted men and women as especially tasty two-legged animals. Once the little man had selected a man or a woman, the victim was doomed unless he feigned death. It was no use trying to hide. Woo could find his prey anywhere. The only way to escape being eaten was to lie on an ant hill and let the ants crawl over eyes and mouth and nose without moving. People who had escaped in this way took the precaution of carrying little bags full of maggots wherever they went. When they saw that Woo was following them, they put a handful of maggots in their hair, and over their faces, and lay down. When Woo saw the maggots he was deceived, thinking that the body was dead.

With his wonderful gift of swift travel, Woo went far away from his home. The giantess who had given birth to him had not seen him for many years, but she heard gruesome stories of his cruelty and vindictive nature.

In old age Woo became dissatisfied and lonely. The reptiles and insects he befriended made use of him, and benefitted by his help, but they could not give him love or affection. No one else had ever been cast in the same mould as Woo, and men and women who might have become his companions lived in terror even of his name.

He roamed restlessly from one place to another. Eventually his one-footed progress brought him back to the foothills of Mount Gambier. He looked up at his mother and held out his arms in a gesture of appeal, but it seemed more like an act of defiance to her.

Her face was set in a frozen mask, furrowed by the tears that had flowed for so many years. Woo could not speak to her. The only word he could say was his own name.

"Woo-oo-oo!" It sounded like the breeze in the leaves of the trees.

The mountain goddess took no notice of the pathetic, eerie sound. Woo's cruelty stood like a barrier between them. Stony-faced, silent, she sat as she had done through all the centuries, while little Woo who loved insects, and would have been a figure of fun if it had not been for his cruel nature, sat down and died of a broken heart.

THE SONG OF THE TREE FROGS

In the days when the Alcooringa or Old People lived on earth, the little Frogs had an unhappy time, living in constant fear of the Snakes which made their homes by the side of billabongs and streams. Their favourite food was Frogs, and the numbers of the little people began to dwindle alarmingly.

The Frogs appealed to the Alcooringa to save them. The Old People felt sorry for them, and forced the Snakes to make their homes in the caves and cracks in the rocks of the hills at some distance from the water. The Snakes were not very happy with this arrangement, because they had a long way to go to drink. The Alcooringa advised them to go by night when it was cool, and when they would not be likely to be attacked by their old enemies the Kookaburras.

"Now," the Alcooringa told the little Frogs, "you will be safe all day long."

"But what about night time?" they wailed. "The Snakes will come and eat us at night!"

"No they won't, not unless you are careless. You can climb up the paper-bark trees and you will be safe from them."

"We can't climb trees!" they cried in unison.

"Have you ever tried?"

"Of course not!"

"Well, try now, little ones."

So the tiny Frogs jumped out of the water and went up to the trees.

"Look!" shouted one of them. "Look at your fingers and toes!"

The Frogs stared in amazement at their hands and feet. Sucker-like discs had grown on the ends of their fingers and toes, and they were able to walk up the tree trunks as easily as if they were logs lying on the ground.

"Oh, thank you, thank you!" they sang.

The song went on for a long time, until they were all tired, and went to sleep in their tree homes.

So the little Tree Frog lives on the bark of trees, hanging on with the suckers that were given to his ancestors by the Alcooringa, and every night he sings his song of thanksgiving to the Old People who saved him from the Snakes.

THE SPEAR WITH THE STINGRAY SPINES

ALTHOUGH he went to catch fish for his family nearly every day, Jigalulu was careful never to wade out into deep water. It had been his custom, after throwing a spear at a fish, to dive into the water to retrieve it, bringing back the fish at the same time. Jigalulu got his wife to twist fibres together to make a long cord which he tied to the handle of the spear. After this he carved barbs at the points of the prongs so that the fish could not escape. In this way he could haul back the spear and whatever was impaled on the prongs without having to go far into the water.

The reason for his caution was a memory he had of the fishing expedition from which his father and two of his brothers had never returned. Some of the elders were of the opinion that they had been swept away by a strong tidal current, but Jigalulu was certain that they had been eaten by a monster that had come in from the deep sea. After that he had always taken care never to go out of his depth and when he stood on the reef he made sure that he would not be washed off by an unexpected wave.

"I know that they were killed and eaten by a monster fish," he said to his wife sometimes when they were talking together at night. "The old men don't know. They never go fishing and they have forgotten all they have learnt. Sometimes I have seen the water swirl and a dim white shape as big as a tree glides under the water. Some day I am going to kill it and avenge the death of my father and brothers."

His wife tried to dissuade him.

"You don't really know what happened to them," she argued. "And even if it was a monster, what could you do? Your father was a famous fisherman and he had his sons with him. You go out alone and have no one to help you. I would rather have a living husband than one who died trying to avenge the death of his family."

Then Jigalulu would say no more, but to himself he muttered that he would kill the monster that ate them.

As he was standing on the reef one day he saw a big stingray swimming past. In a flash his spear ploughed through the water, piercing the body of the big fish. He hauled in the cord. The stingray flapped and struggled to get free, but the barbed prongs held fast, and Jigalulu hauled it slowly up to the surface. Suddenly the water boiled round

his feet and a long grey shape sped through the sea faster than any spear he had ever thrown. He caught a glimpse of white as it turned on its back, a cavernous mouth, and rows of shining teeth. The mouth closed, and the body of the stingray was bitten in two pieces. The huge shape vanished in the depths as Jigalulu dragged the small fragment that was left of the stingray on to the reef.

"I knew it! I knew it!" he shouted. "That is the monster that killed my father!"

He took the small portion of the fish home and walked up and down wondering how he could kill the monster. Overhead Jigalulu the Crane, after whom the fisherman was named, flew past. A thought came into Jigalulu's mind. He knew that Crane had put it there!

"The spines of the stingray will kill the killer of your father and your brothers. There is magic in the spines."

Jigalulu knew what he had to do. In the past there had been many meals of stingray flesh in the camp, and their many sharp spines lying on the midden. It took but a short time to pick up a handful of them. He chose the best ones, polished the long shaft of his spear, stripped off the prongs and lashed the stingray spines firmly to its head, impregnating the threads with gum so that they would not unravel.

He held the spear up to the light, letting the sun shine on it, admiring the gleaming surface, and the way the sunlight twinkled on the white spines.

"This is the instrument of vengeance," he exulted, showing it to his relatives. "There is magic in it."

He ran down to the shore and climbed a rock with a flat top which overhung the water. Holding the spear high above his head he sang and danced the fish dance, the dance that imitated the swift movement of fish in the sea, the shuddering impact of a spear in their bodies, the struggles as they tried to escape, the long, reluctant submission to the man and the spear that overcame them. Words came to him, and song, and the air quivered with the strong magic of the song and the dance. Crane flew round in lazy circles and approved the magic that Jigalulu had made.

The man ran to the edge of the rock and peered over. He was not surprised to see the monster gliding towards him. Vast and menacing it would have been to any other man, but not to Jigalulu on that day of days. Like a flash of forked lightning the spear sang through the air, carrying sunshine and magic with it in its swift flight. A bubble of air floated to the surface of the water, and then the spear was deep in the monster's flesh.

It rose swiftly to the surface and above it like a bird, crashed down again in a smother of foam, and swam round in frenzied circles. The water surged up the rock almost to Jigalulu's feet. In the middle of a seething cauldron the monster tried vainly to twist its head round so that it could bite off the spear that was working its way towards its heart. When it realised that it could not reach the shaft, it hurled itself against the solid rock. The impact nearly dislodged Jigalulu, but he hung grimly to the edge, looking down into the agitated water. Amidst the tattered fragments of weed and yellow foam he saw the great fish smashing its way through coral and waterworn rocks. He saw his beautiful spear break under the impact. The monster turned and sped out to sea with the stingray spines embedded in its back.

Since that day they have always projected above the water in the form of a fin, warning men that Burbangi the Shark is there, enabling them to escape before he can catch them.

SPINY LIZARD AND GALAH BIRD

RED Spiny Lizard, whose name is Oolah, was tired of lying in the sunshine. The land drowsed in the midday heat, and everyone was content to rest. Of all the men, Oolah was the only one who was full of energy. He picked up his boomerangs and admired them. His favourite was the bubbera. It was smaller than the others, better polished, inscribed with exciting designs, and boldly curved. The sun shone on the smooth surface. Oolah felt the satisfying grip of the handle. He threw it so that it skimmed close to the ground, rose into the air in a sweeping curve, and floated lazily back, coming to rest at his feet.

"Very good, Oolah," said a voice. It was the grey Galah Bird who was speaking.

Oolah had never taken much notice of him before. He was such a drab, uninteresting fellow, but no man can resist praise, not even those of the Lizard tribe.

"I can do better than that," he boasted. With all his strength behind it, the bubbera flew across the ground like a blurred puff of wind, and reached a tree on the far side of the clearing, where it severed a leafy twig. Before the leaves could reach the ground the boomerang came towards the two men, faster than the sound of its flight. Oolah ducked, the boomerang sailed over him, and in its wheeling flight it caught the top of Galah's head and lifted his scalp. The blood poured out and ran down his face.

For a moment Galah was stunned. Then with a scream of rage he attacked Oolah. The frightened Lizard crawled on all fours to the shelter of a thorny bush, hoping that Galah would not be able to reach him. It was a vain hope. Galah was so infuriated that he let nothing stop him.

He picked Oolah up in his hands and threw him into the middle of the bush where the thorns stuck into his body.

Oolah screamed with pain. Mercilessly Galah dragged him out, rolling him on the ground until the thorns penetrated Lizard's body so deeply that they could not be pulled out. As he bent over him, the blood from his head ran over Oolah's body. It was only that circumstance that saved Lizard from death. He became so slippery with blood that he was able to wriggle out of Galah's hands.

"That will teach you!" Galah hissed as Oolah ran away. "Red Spiny Lizard! Red blood and thorny spines you will always have to remind you of what you did to me!"

Oolah wriggled between two stones and turned to face Galah.

"You will remember it too, Galah," he jeered. "Old baldy! You will always be bald. That

will teach you to fight me."

Who can say which of them came off worst—Galah with his red, gashed head, or Oolah covered with the spines of the thorn bush?

SUN, MOON, AND THE SPIRIT OF BIRTH

YHI, the sun goddess, fell in love with Bahloo, the moon. She can think of nothing else but the fair, round, silvery face of the moon god, and pursues him endlessly across the sky. When the moon is in eclipse it seems as though his persistent lover will be able to overtake and subdue him, but he always succeeds in escaping. During the hours of daylight Bahloo constantly tries to elude the spirits who live on the horizon and take refuge on the earth, but they are in league with Yhi and turn him back again.

It is only at night that the moon is able to creep past

them. He takes the form of an emu and continues his age-long task of creating girl babies and protecting their mothers. He is the guardian of girls and women, while Boomayah-mayahmul the Wood Lizard is responsible for making boy babies.

Wahn the Crow is Bahloo's chief assistant. When the moon is unable to get back to earth because of the clouds, he takes Bahloo's place, but because he is noisy and quarrelsome, the girl babies he brings into the world have noisy and unpleasant dispositions. For this reason the blacks wait eagerly for Bahloo to return to earth. When he is late in rising, they say, "Bahloo must have been making a lot of babies tonight!"

Waddahgudjaelwon is the spirit of birth. He has the responsibility of placing the spirits of the unborn babies where they will be found by the right mothers, because the real father was not credited with playing any part in the birth of the child. Waddah-gudjaelwon put the infant spirits in hollow trees, streams, rocks, and caves. These places are usually associated with different totems. When the mother came close to the hiding place of the infant spirit, she knew what its totem would be when it was born.

Bahloo had such an important part to play in the birth of a child that mothers were careful not to offend him. If they stared at the moon, Bahloo would be annoyed and would send them twins instead of a single baby. This was a terrible punishment for the mother, for it was a disgrace that could not be lived down. In some parts of New South Wales there are coolabah trees with drooping branches to which the child spirits cling, ready to take up residence in any passing mother. If she was unfortunate enough to stand under a branch where two spirits were suspended, she would become the mother of twins. It was such a disgrace that one of the babies would have to be put to death. The first-born twin came into the world with his tongue protruding, and grinning at its mother's shame.

Because so many unborn spirits were waiting, motherhood could only be avoided with difficulty. Wurrawilberoo, the Whirlwind, for instance, would sometimes take a baby spirit from its hiding place and deposit it in the body of a young woman to whom he had taken a dislike, or perhaps simply in a spirit of mischief. Such babies could always be recognised because they were born with a full set of teeth. When a whirlwind approached an encampment, the young women made themselves scarce at short notice.

Some baby spirits were unable to find a mother. The homeless babies wailed dismally until they were turned into mistletoe plants, the orange flowers of which are stained with their blood.

SUNS, MOONS, AND STARS

BEYOND the horizon, where no one has ever been, there is a beautiful land with grassy valleys and tree-covered hills. Streams trickle down the green slopes and join together to form a broad, placid river, where flowers nod their heads over the banks. The inhabitants of that land are Moons—big, shining, globular Moons. They have no arms or legs, but they can move quickly across the grass by rolling over and over. It is a pleasant life in that green, watered land, but sometimes the Moons grow restless, and when night comes they have the urge to explore farther afield and stroll across the sky.

Only one Moon ever goes on such a journey at a time. It is a pity that they do not go in company, but they do not know that outside the valley there lives a giant. He catches the wandering Moon, and with his flint knife he cuts a slice from it each night, until after many nights there is nothing left but a number of shining slivers. The giant cuts them up very finely and throws them all over the sky.

They are timid little creatures, the cut-up Moons which have become Stars. During the day, when a Sun goes striding across the sky, they hide. Who knows but that, if they showed themselves then, another Sun might not creep out and catch them unawares.

At night there are no Suns, and who cares about the next silly old Moon who will go for a stroll and never come back? Very soon he too will be cut up into Stars. So, in the velvety blackness of the night, they frolic and play until the hungry Sun again stamps across the sky.

TURTLE, OYSTER, AND WHALE

Oyster was married to Sea Turtle. For a time they lived happily together, but after a while Turtle grew tired of her husband's incessant demands. He was sitting huddled up on the beach with his head touching his knees, expecting her to do all the work.

"Hurry up, wife," he called. "I'm thirsty. I want you to dig a well in the sand."

Turtle looked at him coldly.

"You have as many hands as I have," she said in a shrill voice.

"Never mind how many hands I have," Oyster retorted. "Get to work with your own and dig that well for me."

She stood over him and spread out her hands.

"Two hands for cutting firewood," she said. "Two hands for making a fire. Two hands for building the wurley. Two hands for cooking the morning meal. What hands will I use for digging a well? It's time you used your two hands to do some work."

Oyster jumped up and hit her on the face and body.

"Two hands to hit you with," he mocked her. "How do you like that, little Turtle wife?"

Miintinta the Turtle woman didn't like it at all. She picked up her husband and dumped him on the sand so hard that he nearly broke in two. He caught her by the neck and dragged her down. They rolled over and over on the sand, hitting and kicking and making so much noise that Akama the Whale heard it. He was travelling up the coast and turned aside to see what was happening.

He looked down at them with a smile. He was a big man. Two enormous hands picked up Oyster and Turtle and held them apart.

"You are old enough to know better than to fight like wild animals," he reproved them. "There, see if you can behave yourselves now," and he put them on their feet.

Never before had Whale been so surprised. Forgetting all about her husband, Turtle flew at him, biting and scratching, while Oyster picked up a digging stick and hit him on the back.

"What have I done?" Whale cried. "I was only trying to help you."

"Then get away as fast as you can and never interfere again between husband and wife."

Akama looked at them with a puzzled expression.

"All right!" he said hastily as Oyster took a step towards him, and he ran away as fast as his legs would carry him.

Whale never stops on his long trip up the coast now, for he has learned to mind his own business. Turtle is still busy with her hands, digging in the soft, warm sand and laying her eggs in the holes she makes.

WHY CURLEW CRIES PLAINTIVELY AT NIGHT

OOYAN the Curlew has thin red legs and cries incessantly at night, but in the beginning of time, when he was still a man, he was plump and happy. Too plump, too good-natured, and above all, too lazy. While other young men were out foraging for food, Ooyan stayed by the camp fire or lay in the sunshine, getting in the way of the women. He was so good-natured that they did not hesitate to tell him what they thought of him, knowing that he would be too lazy to strike them when they insulted him.

"You are not a man," they jeered. "A real man goes out to get food for his family. He knows that his life depends on his skill with spear and boomerang. You are not even a woman. You won't look for yams. Look, here is a yam stick. See if you can use it."

Ooyan brushed it lazily to one side.

"I am quite happy where I am," he said. "It is your job to find food for me."

His wife was furious. "If you won't dig for yams I can find another use for my yam stick,"

she threatened.

She began to beat him with her stick. Ooyan got up and retreated behind a tree, but she followed him, hitting him with all her strength.

Smarting from the blows, and realising that at last she was in earnest, Ooyan snatched up a stone knife and a spear and ran out of the camp. All day he hunted for game, but he had no skill, and try as he might, he could not come within striking distance of the animals that bounded away as soon as he came near them.

He knew that he would suffer further indignities if he returned to the women without any food, and that they would make him the laughing stock of the tribe. His days of indolence were over, and somehow he must prove his manhood. The stone knife that dangled from his belt attracted his attention. On a sudden impulse he drew it from its sheath, fingered the sharp edge, and plunged it into his leg, carving a large piece of flesh from it. He wrapped it in leaves and hobbled home. When he came in sight of the camp he adjusted his kangaroo skin so that it covered the bleeding part of his leg.

"Here you are," he said to his wife. "Cook this and say nothing about it."

He refused to eat any of it himself, but watched the others as they devoured the cooked meat.

"What is it?" they asked him. "It tastes different to any meat that we have eaten."

"Never mind," he said. "You told me to get you some food. Are you complaining when I bring you meat you have never tasted before?"

He curled himself up in his skin rug in the gunyah.

"You did very well," his wife said as he was drifting off to sleep. "I felt proud of you tonight for once. You must go out again tomorrow."

"I will hunt no more," he said sullenly.

"Oh yes, you will. You have shown that you can hunt with the best of them. I am tired of being ashamed of you. If you lie in the sun when other men are hunting I will give you a touch of my yam stick again."

Poor Ooyan's leg had stiffened by morning, but he was forced out of the encampment by his wife. Once again he found that he could not get close to his prey, and to save himself from further punishment, he had to take a slice from the other leg. He could scarcely stagger back to the camp for weakness and loss of blood.

After the evening meal, which again he left untasted, he was unable to get up.

"What is the matter with you?" asked one of the women. "Get up and join in the dance."

Ooyan groaned. The woman became impatient. She snatched his kangaroo skin from him, and everyone could see the gaping wounds in his legs. They uttered a cry of horror.

"He has fed us with his own flesh!" they exclaimed.

They had no pity for Ooyan. The women picked up their yam sticks and drove him out into the darkness, where all night long he cried with pain and misery.

So it was that Ooyan turned into a Curlew with thin, red, fleshless legs, who cries because he is lonely in the darkness.

136

THE WINDS

THERE were six winds, three of which were male, and three female. The cold west wind is called Gheeger Gheeger. She is guarded by Wahn the Crow, who keeps her confined in a hollow log. It is necessary for him to do this because she has such a turbulent nature. Sometimes she escapes, and Wahn is kept busy trying to catch her and bring her back. The log is slowly decaying. When it finally falls to pieces, Wahn will be unable to control the west wind, which will run wild, and will devastate the whole earth.

The south wind, Gooroondoodilbaydilbay, is accompanied by Mullian the Eagle Hawk, who can be seen in the sky riding on her back in the form of towering cumulus clouds.

The south-east wind, Yarrageh, has three wives, the Budtha, Bibbil, and Bumble trees. When he makes love to them, they begin to grow and put forth flowers and fruit as a sign that Yarrageh, the spirit of spring, has arrived.

The north wind, Douran Douran, is also a great lover. From his kisses come the floral dresses of the Coolah, Noongah, and Kurrajong trees.

The east wind is Gunyahmoo.

Twice a year there is a corroboree which is attended by all the winds, including Gheeger Gheeger, who is released for this special occasion by Wahn The female winds are unpredictable and wild. They rage through the trees, breaking branches and moaning because their lovers have been stolen from them. In contrast to their behaviour, the male winds, with the exception of Gheeger Gheeger, are gentle. It is their love which causes trees to put on their leaves, and to flower and fruit, and the earth to blossom in its green mantle.

THE WOMAN WHO CHANGED INTO A KANGAROO

A WOMAN's life is hard and monotonous. While her husband has the freedom of the plains and the bush, and the excitement of the chase, she has to seek all day long for grubs, or dig with her yam stick to find edible roots. At night there is the meal to prepare, children to care for, and a thousand and one other things to do if she is to keep her husband contented.

There was once a woman who rebelled against this life of toil. Abandoning her children, she left the camp while her husband was away hunting, and ran across the level ground until she came to the hills, where there was a stream of water and a pleasant valley in which she could shelter from the cold night wind. She dared not light a fire lest her hiding place should be discovered, but she had her bag filled with cooked roots, grubs, and flesh. She stayed in the valley for several days. Sometimes she climbed to the top of the hill and looked across the plain. One day she saw a tiny black thing like an ant moving across it, and knew it was her husband. She grinned in triumph, because she knew she had concealed her tracks so carefully that he would never find her.

After many days had passed she decided that he must have given up the search. Her provision bag was empty except for the fire-making sticks she had brought with her. She had no hunting weapons, nor the skill to use them, but there were many edible roots in the valley, green vegetables, and fat grubs to provide her with flesh food. That night the fire glowed cheerfully by the stream, and when she had eaten to repletion she lay beside the embers and felt the warmth seeping through her body.

Her husband had not given up the search. He was camped close to the foothills. He saw the glow of the fire in the distance, and again in the morning there was a narrow thread of smoke rising from the trees beckoning to him.

The sun was high when he reached the sheltered valley. He hid behind a rock and watched his wife lifting the loose bark from the trunks of trees, searching for her favourite grubs. With a pleased smile he stepped out of his hiding place and began to walk towards her. The woman shrieked and fled to the shelter of a clump of trees with her husband in hot pursuit. She was fleet of foot and managed to get some distance ahead of him.

The broken stump of a tree gave promise of a hiding

place. She crouched behind it, grasping it in her arms and pressing her body against it. Her husband had lost sight of her, but he was able to follow her footprints. They wound between the trees and led up to the stump. For a moment he was puzzled, because the stump was in the open and he could not see his wife, who was hiding behind it. He looked more carefully and could discern her black arms silhouetted against the white trunk where the bark had dropped off.

He walked towards her confidently, but he had not reckoned with the magic words she had remembered. As he made his leisurely approach across the grass there was a sharp crack. The tree lifted itself from the ground and, with the woman still clinging to it, progressed in leaps and bounds, and in a few moments disappeared down the valley. The man ran until the blood pounded in his ears and his breath came in great gasps, but he could not catch up with the leaping tree. He was forced to watch it hopping across the plain until it was lost to sight.

Every time you see a Kangaroo leaping on its strong legs, and think of this tale of long ago, you will realise that all kangaroos must have descended from the woman who grasped the white tree and leaped with it to safety. She did not know the spells that would release her, and she went on jumping until the tea-tree stump became part of her, until her legs grew long, and her arms became short and wizened because they had nothing to do except to keep the tree pressed close to her body.

But if you look for a moral in the story, perhaps the only thing you can find will be that wives should not run away from their husbands.

In a tiny clearing in the thickest part of the bush where no one could see him, Djarapa worked busily all day, absorbed in his work. It would have been easy to have taken a fallen branch, but Djarapa needed living wood for the work he had to do. He felled a tree and lopped off the top and the branches. The trunk was taller than a man and as thick as two men standing together. He had selected four branches, and each branch was cut in two pieces.

They were lying on the ground in the shape of a man, but Djarapa was not satisfied. There was something wrong with them. Then he realised that his wooden man had no head. It was a long time before he could find a way to make a head, but when the spirits put a thought into his own head, he shouted with delight. Holding his flint knife firmly in his hand, he chipped at one end of the trunk until it took the shape of a head separated from the body by a thin neck.

He had spent many days at work on his wooden man, but the hardest part still lay before him. Holes had to be bored through the ends of the arms and legs, and tied on to the body with cords of human hair. He hollowed out the sockets and fitted them with water-worn stones for joints. He had already cut off his wife's hair, and with infinite patience he stuck the hairs one by one to the top of the wooden head.

All that remained was to place two painted pebbles in sockets that he had gouged out of the face, and teeth in the cavernous mouth, and to daub the body with white and yellow clay.

"My Wulgaru!" Djarapa whispered proudly. "The man-thing I have made with my own hands need only breath and life to make him walk like a warrior."

He chanted the most powerful incantations he knew, and tapped the figure with his woomera. The sun sank, dusk changed to dark and, daring the evil spirits of the night, Djarapa chanted and tapped without stopping—on through the night and the dim light of dawn, on through the morning song of birds and the growing daylight, on and on as the sunlight dappled the ground under the trees; and all the time the Wulgaru lay motionless, unresponsive to the chanting, staring upwards with its stony eyes.

Long shadows of the late afternoon lay across the tiny clearing. Djarapa straightened himself slowly and painfully. In a fit of petulance he kicked the wooden figure and walked along the track to his camp.

"Thud, thud, thud!"

He stopped and listened, but could hear nothing; but as soon as he began walking again, he could hear the unusual thudding noise. He stopped for a second time, and the noise ceased. His senses thoroughly roused, he walked on, moving silently with his ears strained to catch the slightest sound. He heard it again. It was a mixture of noises—heavy footsteps, a grating sound like wood and stone rubbing together, a ringing clash like the teeth of a crocodile when he misses his prey, a breaking of branches and rustling of leaves. The path lay straight in front of him. Djarapa marched steadily along it without turning his head. When he came to the end he whirled round and saw his Wulgaru striding towards him. The wooden figure

was snapping its jaws and crashing through the overhanging branches. It came to a halt, and in its stony eyes there was a malevolence that chilled Djarapa's heart.

So there began a long chase in which Djarapa the woodcarver was hunted by the thing he had created. Relentlessly it pursued him. Djarapa's brain was racing faster than his feet. He turned a corner, and in the few moments that he was out of sight of his pursuer, he plunged into a screen of foliage and took shelter behind the trunk of a tree. Peeping cautiously from his hiding place,

141

he saw the Wulgaru running past. Startled birds flew from its path. The wooden hands clutched at them, the teeth-studded jaws clattered and clashed as loudly as the stone joints in his legs.

Djarapa followed at a distance, wondering what would happen when the wooden man reached the bank of the river. The Wulgaru did not hesitate. It stepped off the bank and sank lower and lower into the water until it disappeared from sight. The man heaved a sigh of relief. He knew that the Wulgaru he had made would kill and devour him if it was able to catch him. He was about to turn away when a movement on the far bank of the river caught his eye. It was the Wulgaru climbing out of the water. It had walked across the bed of the river, unharmed by the water, and went on its way.

Djarapa hurried back to his camp and told the incredible story to his tribespeople. The fires burnt brightly that night, and everyone lived in fear, as well they might, for neither fire nor water, spear nor magic spell could harm the Wulgaru.

It is a living man, but it does not breathe; it is a devil-devil, but it has the form of a man; it is only the trunk of a tree and a few river stones, but it has life and movement. It is Wulgaru, the devil-devil which still lives, and will live for ever, the devil-devil which kills men and women and children who break the tribal laws, but which has never been known to touch those who obey.

YARA-MA-YHA-WHO

"LITTLE children, beware of the Yara-ma-yha-who! If you do not behave yourselves and do as you are told, they will come and eat you. Then you will be turned into Yara-ma-yha-whos yourselves, and what could be worse than that!

"Let us tell you what they are like. They are no bigger than you, but they have big heads and stomachs—so big that they are nearly all head and stomach. Their jaws are not hinged at the back, so that they can open them wide and swallow boys and girls as big as themselves. They can even swallow men and women! They have suckers on the ends of their fingers and toes for holding on with, and they are red all over—red hair, red skin, and big, glaring, red eyes. They live in trees, and if children are naughty, these horrible little men will drop down from the branches and swallow them up."

"But if they eat only naughty children, why are men and women afraid of them?"

"That is why we are so afraid of them. It wouldn't be so bad if it was only the naughty children, but remember, the naughtier you are now, the more likely it is that the Yara-ma-yha-who will come creeping up to you and hold you tight with their suckers. Then —whee—their mouths will open and you will disappear right into their stomachs."

"Tell us more about them." the children said, huddling close to the fire, and casting apprehensive glances over their shoulders. "Who has seen the Yara-ma-yha-who?"

"I have!"

The high-pitched, quavering voice came from the old grand-mother.

"Your uncle was turned into a Yara-ma-yha-who!"

The children shrank closer to their mothers' sides.

"Your uncle had been out hunting, and he was very tired. He lay down to rest in the shade of a tree, and before he could call out, a Yara-ma-yha-who leaped on him and sucked his blood with the little suckers on his fingers and toes."

The biggest and bravest of the boys sneered.

"Then he must be dead, grandmother!"

"Oh no. The Yara-ma-yha-who left some blood in him. The little man lay flat on the ground, opened his mouth as wide as he could (and that was very wide), and crept right over him until my son disappeared into his stomach."

"How do you know all this, grandmother?" someone asked.

"Because I saw it with my own two eyes."

"Then why didn't you try to save him?"

Granny laughed, a high-pitched laughter that made everybody shiver.

"I saw it all happen, but I was a long way off. I took my husband's war spear and ran as quickly as I could, but long before I could reach him, the Yara-ma-yha-who stood up, danced up and down, and then ran off to a water hole, where he drank and drank. I was very close to him when he saw me. He held his huge stomach, with your uncle inside it, with his hands, and ran away so quickly that I lost him.

"Now listen to me, because what I am going to tell you will be very important to you if ever you are caught by a Yara-ma-yha-who. After he has swallowed you and drunk plenty of water, he will lie on the ground and bring up his meal. You will still be alive. You must keep quite still and the Yara-ma-yha-who will think you are dead. He will try to make sure. He will poke you and tickle you, and if you don't move, he will go away and hide. If you lie quite still until it is dark, he will go to sleep and you will be able to escape."

"Why didn't our uncle do that?"

The old lady looked mournfully into the fire.

"He didn't know what I am telling you now. I think he tried to run away. That means that the Yara-ma-yha-who caught him. By that time he would have been easier to swallow, because by then he would have become smaller. I expect that the creature brought him up a second time, and swallowed him again. By that time he would have been no bigger than the Yara-ma-yha-who. If we had been there we would have seen him slowly turning red, his head growing big, his stomach growing big, his legs becoming smaller, suckers growing on his fingers and toes until he became a . . ."

"Yara-ma-yha-who!" the children shrieked.

"But what if he had escaped? How do you know he didn't escape and run away to some other place?"

"Because he never came back. If he had escaped, the Yara-ma-yha-who would have been angry. They would have drunk all the water in the water holes, and we would have had to get water from wild apple trees and from mallee roots."

"See that you behave yourselves," all the mothers whispered, as the children lay down to sleep. "See what will happen to you if you don't!"